New York State

May to May Mathematics

Continental

Acknowledgments

Photo Credits: Front cover and title page: www.istockphoto.com/nicolecioe

ISBN 978-0-8454-6960-6

Welcome to New York State May to May Mathematics!

Mathematics is more than numbers. It's more than knowing how to add, subtract, multiply, and divide. You use math when you estimate if you have enough money to buy something. You use it when you recognize the pattern in the beat of music. It helps you understand a graph in the newspaper and how to use a ruler to measure the width of your desk.

This book was written to help you get ready for the New York State mathematics test. Why do you need it? You've been studying math ever since you started school. As you get close to a test, the best way to prepare is to review the ideas and practice the skills you will need for it.

New York State May to May Mathematics contains lessons to review the things you have learned in math class. Each lesson includes examples to show you what the idea means or how the skill is used. On the right side of the lesson page is a sidebar. It contains hints and reminders of things that are related to the main idea of the lesson. After each lesson, there are problems to help you practice what you have reviewed.

The practice pages have several kinds of problems. That's because the real New York State test has more than one kind of question. The problems in this book will help you find out what you know about math ideas, skills, and problem solving. Just as on real math tests, some of the problems in this book are very easy. Others may make you think a bit. And a few will be a challenge.

- The first practice page has **multiple-choice** problems. These problems give you four answers to choose from. In each lesson of this book, the first problem is always a sample. A box under this item tells you how to find the correct answer.

  When you answer a multiple-choice question, be sure to read all the answer choices carefully before choosing one. Some answers can be tricky.

- The next page has **short-response** questions that you must answer in writing. Each one has two parts. In the first part, you usually need to figure out the solution to the problem. You may be asked to show your work. Or you might need to write a short answer or draw a diagram. In the second part, you will have to identify your solution or explain why your answer is correct. You may need to describe the steps you took to find it.

The first short-response problem is a sample. A box under it explains the answer and how to find it. The second problem you must do on your own.

To answer a writing question, follow the item directions exactly. Ask yourself, "Am I answering the question that is being asked?" Always think about what you will say before writing an explanation. Your thoughts should be clear and organized. Your writing should be neat so it can be read. If you are asked to show your work, be sure the steps are easy to follow and your answer is labeled.

• The last page of practice has an extended-response problem. This is the same kind of problem as the short-response items, but it is longer. Often, an extended-response item has three parts. Occasionally it will have only two parts, but each of those parts may call for a little more work than usual. For example, an extended-response question might ask you to make a graph or draw a geometric figure.

At the end of each unit are three pages of review problems. The problems in this section cover all the lessons in that unit, in a mixed order. The review includes all three types of problems you worked with in the lessons: multiple-choice, short-response, and extended-response problems.

A practice test, glossary, and a set of flash cards are at the end of this book. The practice test addresses all the skills you have reviewed. It is set up just like the real New York State test. The glossary lists important terms and their definitions. The flash cards show some of the important math ideas you have reviewed. Cut out the flash cards so you can review these ideas. Practice by yourself or with a friend. There are blank flash cards so you can make some of your own!

Understanding Mathematical Processes

Learning mathematics has two parts. One part is **mathematical content.** Content includes the skills and ideas you use when you add numbers, read the fractions on a ruler, recognize a triangle, find information on a graph, or weigh something on a scale.

Another equally important part is **mathematical processes.** These are the skills you use to help you understand and apply the ideas in the content areas. You use them when you explain these ideas to others. And you especially use them when you solve problems.

There are many process skills, and they often overlap. Process skills include:

- **Representation**
- **Connections**
- **Communication**
- **Reasoning and Proof**
- **Problem Solving**

All of these process skills are important in helping you to master mathematical content. They are tied together with content skills—you can't really learn them separately. As you work through a math problem, you may use several process and content skills. This is especially true when you are answering a open-ended question like a short- or extended-response problem.

For example, suppose you are asked to solve a word problem and explain why your answer is correct. You use a problem-solving strategy to figure out the answer. If you write a number sentence to show the mathematics of the word problem, you are using representation. To justify your answer, you use reasoning and proof skills. If you mention a general mathematical rule to prove your answer, you are showing connections. And the written explanation, using the appropriate mathematics vocabulary, demonstrates your communication skills.

The problems in this book are just like those on the actual test. So you will practice both content skills and process skills as you work through the lessons in this book.

In the following sections, you'll see some examples of the kinds of problems that use these process skills.

Representation

Representation problems may ask you to create a model to show a mathematical idea or to organize and record information. Or you might have to choose the correct representation or explain what a model means. These representations can take many forms: pictures, diagrams, models, tallies, graphs, geometric figures, number sentences, patterns, and more.

Here's an example of a problem that calls for representation skills.

Vin ate $\frac{1}{3}$ of a pizza. Draw and label a picture to show $\frac{1}{3}$.

This problem asks you to model a mathematical idea, the fraction $\frac{1}{3}$. The clue is the word *Draw*. Consider what you know about the fraction $\frac{1}{3}$. The number on the bottom is the denominator and it tells you how many equal parts there are—3. The number on the top is the numerator and it tells you how many parts are being talked about—1. A pizza is usually a circle, so you can draw a circle, divide it into 3 equal parts, and shade 1 of them. Remember to label the shaded part! Here's what your response might look like.

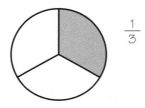

Connections

Connections problems may ask you to recognize how mathematical ideas are related or build on each other. Or you may need to use a related idea to solve a problem. Sometimes you need to apply a mathematical connection to a real-life situation. You may need to show how mathematics is part of everyday life.

Here's an example of a problem that calls for connections skills.

What number goes in the box to make this number sentence true?

$$5 + \square = 7$$

This problem asks you to find a missing number in an addition sentence. You may remember that addition and subtraction are related. They are inverse, or opposite, operations. So you can use this connection to solve the problem. You think:

"5 plus some number is 7. That's the same as 7 minus 5 is…2."

Communication

Mathematical ideas are most useful when they can be shared. Problems that practice your communication skills may ask you to explain how you solved a problem or why an answer is correct. You may be asked to express a mathematical idea, using the words and phrases that make up mathematical language. To do well on these problems, you should be able to organize your thoughts clearly. You should also know the meanings of mathematical words so you can use them correctly.

Here's an example of a problem that calls for connections skills.

How are a rectangle and a square alike and different?

To answer this question, you must know the meanings of the words *rectangle* and *square*. You will have learned these words when you studied geometric figures. You might write a response like this:

Rectangles and squares are geometric shapes. They are alike because they both have four sides and four square corners. They are different because the square has sides that are all the same length. The rectangle can have one pair of opposite sides that are a different length than the other pair of sides.

Reasoning and Proof

Understanding *why* is just as important as understanding *how* in mathematics. Problems that focus on reasoning skills may ask you to prove that a mathematical statement is true or false. To do this, you should be able to think logically about the idea and to provide examples to justify your argument. Often you will rely on mathematical connections to support your thoughts. Understanding and using mathematical vocabulary correctly also matters. Here again, organizing your thoughts is important. A proof is easiest to understand when it leads from one step to the next.

Here's an example of a problem that calls for reasoning and proof skills.

Layla says that the sum of two odd numbers is always odd. Is Layla right? Why or why not?

To decide if Layla is right, test some examples of her statement. Pick some odd numbers and add them to see whether their sums are odd or even. For example: $3 + 5 = 8, 5 + 7 = 12, 7 + 9 = 16, 25 + 25 = 50$. All these examples produced sums that are even, so Layla is not right. To respond to this kind of question, start with a general statement. Then produce your examples as evidence. You might write something like this:

Layla is not correct. When two odd numbers are added, the sum is even. I tested some examples: $3 + 5 = 8$ and $7 + 9 = 16$. Every odd number is an even number plus 1. So adding two odd numbers is the same as adding two even numbers $+ 1 + 1$. So the sum of two odd numbers will always be even.

Problem Solving

Some mathematics problems test your understanding of mathematical ideas. Others test your skills in computation or other procedures. But many problems call for more than just recalling a fact or doing a calculation. They require you to analyze a situation and figure out a way to find an answer. They may be word problems, but they can be other types of problems, like geometry, too. You need to be able to put your different skills together to solve a problem.

You should know and be able to use the **four-step problem-solving procedure.**

1. **Read** the problem. What is the question? What kind of information does the problem give? To be sure you understand the problem, you can restate it in your own words.

2. **Plan** how to find a solution. What steps must you take? What calculations must you make? Does the problem have all the information you need or is something missing? Is there information in the problem that is not needed and that you can ignore? What strategy will you use? To develop a plan, identify the steps you must take to solve the problem.

3. **Solve** the problem. Do you need to show your work? Be careful to carry out your plan in a clear, step-by-step fashion. Ask yourself if someone else could follow your steps.

4. **Check** your answer. Does it make sense? Think about your answer in light of the question that was asked. If the answer does not make sense, go back and try again.

You should also know and be able to use a variety of **problem-solving strategies.** Some strategies you should be familiar with are listed here.

- Guess and check
- Draw a picture or diagram
- Look for a pattern
- Reason it out
- Make a table or a list
- Work backward
- Break it into steps
- Write a number sentence
- Work a simpler problem

Here's an example of a word problem test item that calls for problem-solving skills.

José and two friends are going to the movies. The price of a child's ticket is $7.00. The price of an adult's ticket is $8.50. The three third graders have a total of $30. How much money will they have left for snacks after they pay for the tickets? Show your work.

To solve this problem, read it carefully and make a plan for solving it. The friends are third graders, so you need to find the price of three children's tickets. The price of an adult's ticket is just extra information. Find the price of the child's ticket in the problem.

Decide on the operation to use. You could add $7 three times or multiply $7 by 3. Then you will need to find how much money is left after the total is subtracted from $30. Once you have your plan, carry out your work and check it. Your response might look like this.

$$\begin{array}{rr} \$7 & \$30 \\ \times 3 & -21 \\ \hline \$21 & \$\ 9 \end{array}$$

The friends will have $9 left for snacks.

Many problems require not only the problem-solving skills, but all the process skills—reasoning, connections, representation, and communication. You'll be using all of these skills in this book as you work through the lessons and practice problems in each of the content strands.

11

Unit 1
Whole Numbers and Fractions

Numbers are all around you. You use numbers to count the cookies in a bag. You use numbers to show your age. You could skip count to find the number of socks in a pile. Fractions are a type of number. You might think of a fraction when you eat a piece of pie. This unit will help you understand whole numbers and fractions.

Lesson 1 **Whole Numbers** reviews how to write whole numbers in different ways. You will also compose and decompose numbers. You will skip count, too.

Lesson 2 **Place Value** reviews how to find the value of a digit in a number. You will also write numbers in expanded form.

Lesson 3 **Comparing and Ordering Whole Numbers** reviews how to put numbers in order. You will decide which number is greater and which number is less.

Lesson 4 **Understanding Fractions** reviews fractions as part of a whole and as part of a set. You will use models and pictures to find fractions.

Whole Numbers

Indicators   3.N.1, 2, 5

✓ **Whole numbers** are used to count.

$$0, 1, 2, 3, 4, 5, \ldots 10, \ldots 100, \ldots 1{,}000$$

You can name whole numbers in different forms.

- **standard form**   687

- **word form**   six hundred eighty-seven

✓ A whole number can be **composed** or **decomposed** in many different ways.

$$70 + 10 = 80 \qquad\qquad 90 - 10 = 80$$
$$80 = 85 - 5 \qquad\qquad 80 = 20 + 20 + 20 + 20$$

All of these name the whole number 80.

✓ You can use a **number line** to **skip count.**

To count by 25's, add 25 to a number to find which number comes next.

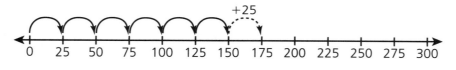

$$150 + 25 = 175$$

To count by 50's, keep adding 50.

$$500 + 50 = 550 \qquad 550 + 50 = 600 \qquad 600 + 50 = 650$$

To count by 100's, keep adding 100.

$$100, 200, 300, 400, 500, \ldots$$

Remember—

You can show whole numbers with a model.

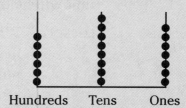

Hundreds   Tens   Ones

This model shows 687.

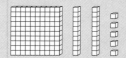

This model shows 125.

Compose means "to make up" or "to put together."

Decompose means "to take apart" or "to break down."

You can use any operation to compose or decompose numbers.

$$2 + 3 = 5$$
$$8 - 3 = 5$$
$$1 \times 5 = 5$$
$$10 \div 2 = 5$$

You can skip count by any number.

By 2's:
    2, 4, 6, 8, 10, …

By 3's:
    3, 6, 9, 12, 15, …

By 4's:
    4, 8, 12, 16, 20, …

By 5's:
    5, 10, 15, 20, 25, …

Unit 1 Whole Numbers and Fractions

Read each problem. Circle the letter of the best answer.

1 Anita is counting by 25's. Which is the first number she says after 250?

   A 255   **C** 300

   B 275   **D** 350

> The correct answer is B. To find the next number, add 25 to the last number Anita said: 250 + 25 = 275.

2 The Iroquois lived in longhouses that were about 200 feet long. What is another way of writing 200?

   A 2 × 10

   B 300 − 200

   C 2 + 100 + 100

   D 50 + 50 + 50 + 50

3 Eight hundred five students go to the Miller Street School. How is this number written in standard form?

   A 85

   B 508

   C 805

   D 850

4 Jake is counting by 50's, starting with 600. Which sentence is true about the next two numbers he will say?

   A He will say 625 and 675.

   B He will say 675 and 700.

   C He will say 650 and 700.

   D He will say 705 and 750.

5 Which choice shows a way of making 900?

   A 1,000 − 100   **C** 700 + 300

   B 800 − 100   **D** 500 + 500

6 Look at this sign.

Entering
Riverwood

975 People

How many people live in Riverwood?

   A nine thousand, nine hundred seventy-five

   B nine hundred fifty-seven

   C ninety-five

   D nine hundred seventy-five

7 Which choice is **not** a way of showing 70?

   A 100 − 10 − 20

   B 50 + 10 + 10

   C 20 + 30 + 30

   D 90 − 10 − 10

8 Paula is counting by 100's. If she starts at 50, which will be the next three numbers she says?

   A 150, 250, 350

   B 100, 200, 300

   C 100, 150, 200

   D 150, 200, 250

Read each problem. Write your answers.

9 Joanne counted to 200 and wanted to continue.

   Part A

   If Joanne is skip counting by 50's, what numbers will she say to count to 400?

   Answer: 250, 300, 350, 400

   Part B

   Explain how you found your answer.

   To count by 50's, just add 50 to the last number Joanne said: 200 + 50 = 250. Continue adding until you reach 400: 250 + 50 = 300, 300 + 50 = 350, 350 + 50 = 400.

10 Warren packed 125 books into three different boxes. He does not know how many books are in each box.

   Show two ways Warren can make 125 using three numbers.

   Answer 1: _____

   Answer 2: _____

Unit 1 Whole Numbers and Fractions

Read the problem. Write your answer for each part.

11 Ms. Johnson's third-grade class collected cans for recycling.

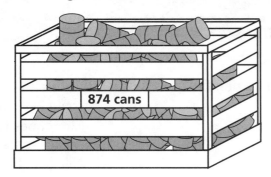

874 cans

Part A

What is this number in words?

Answer: _____

_____

Ask Yourself
Does the word name begin with the hundreds or the ones?

Part B

Lou heard that another class collected nine hundred six cans. He wrote 960 on his paper. Was Lou correct?

Answer: _____

Explain how you know.

_____

_____

_____

_____

Indicator   3.N.4

✅ The value of a digit depends on its place in a number. This is its **place value.**

THOUSANDS	HUNDREDS	TENS	ONES
	3	8	6

In this number, the value of the 3 is 3 hundreds, or 300.

The value of the 8 is 8 tens, or 80.

The value of the 6 is 6 ones, or 6.

✅ A number can be shown in **expanded form.**

$$200 + 40 + 9 = 249$$

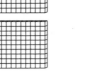

2 hundreds	+	4 tens	+	9 ones
200	+	40	+	9

> *Remember—*
>
> The value of each place is ten times the value of the place to its right.
>
> 5 tens
> ↓
> 555
> ↑ ↑
> 5 hundreds 5 ones
>
> 10 ones = 1 ten
> 10 tens = 1 hundred
> 10 hundreds = 1 thousand

Unit 1 Whole Numbers and Fractions

Read each problem. Circle the letter of the best answer.

1 What is the value of the 5 in 357?

   A 5

   B 50

   C 500

   D 5,000

> The correct answer is B. From right to left, the places are the ones, the tens, and the hundreds. The 5 is in the tens place, so its value is 5 tens, or 50.

2 Long Island is about 120 miles long. How is this written in expanded form?

   A 1 + 2 + 0

   B 1 + 20

   C 100 + 2

   D 100 + 20

3 Which number does this picture show?

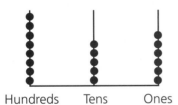

Hundreds   Tens   Ones

   A 865   **C** 685

   B 856   **D** 658

4 Which number is the same as 700 + 20 + 1?

   A 172   **C** 712

   B 217   **D** 721

5 In which number does the 8 have a value of 800?

   A 485

   B 845

   C 548

   D 380

6 Look at the number on this sign.

DAYSTAR FARM
725 acres

The sign painter made a mistake. The digits in the ones and the hundreds places were switched. What should the number on the sign be?

   A 752

   B 572

   C 527

   D 275

7 What number does this picture show?

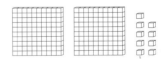

   A 29

   B 209

   C 290

   D 902

Read each problem. Write your answers.

8 The Erastus Corning Tower is a famous tall building in Albany. Its height in feet is a three-digit number with a 9 in the ones place, an 8 in the tens place, and a 5 in the hundreds place.

Part A

How tall is the Erastus Corning Tower?

Answer: _____589_____ feet

Part B

Explain why your answer is correct.

From left to right, the places in a three-digit number are the hundreds, the tens, and the ones. To write this number, put the digits in the correct order. The 5 goes in the hundreds place on the left. Next comes the tens digit, the 8. Finally, the ones digit goes on the right.

9 Look at these base 10 blocks. They show a number.

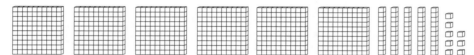

Part A

Write the number shown in standard form.

Answer: _____

Part B

Express this number in expanded form.

Answer: _____

Read the problem. Write your answer for each part.

10 Jill wrote these digits on slips of paper. Then she placed them in this order.

Part A

What is this number written in expanded form?

Answer: _____

Part B

Jill rearranges the digits in another order. What is the **largest** possible number Jill can make with these digits?

Answer: _____

Ask Yourself
Which digit is largest? Which place has the greatest value?

Part C

On the lines below, explain how you know this is the largest possible number.

_____

_____

_____

_____

Comparing and Ordering Whole Numbers

Indicator 3.N.3

✔ To **compare** or **order** whole numbers, look at the digits in the same places, starting on the left.

Beth has 678 pennies in a jar. Barry has 697 pennies in a jar. Who has more pennies?

First line up the numbers. Then start by looking at the digits in the hundreds place.

678
697

The hundreds digits are the same. Look at the tens digits.

6**7**8
6**9**7

These digits are different: 7 is less than 9. So 678 is less than 697, and 697 is greater than 678.

678 < 697 or 697 > 678

Barry has more pennies than Beth.

Sometime the tens digits are the same, too. In that case, look at the ones.

84**4** > 84**3**

844 is greater than 843.

Unit 1 Whole Numbers and Fractions

Read each problem. Circle the letter of the best answer.

1 Which number goes in the box to make this number sentence true?

$$\square > 47$$

A 38   **C** 47

B 46   **D** 54

The correct answer is D. The symbol > means "is greater than." So you need to find a number that is greater than 47. Choices A and B are less than 47. Choice C is equal to 47. Only choice D is greater than 47.

2 On Monday, 226 students ate in the school lunchroom. On Tuesday, a greater number of students ate lunch there. How many students could there have been on Tuesday?

A 219   **C** 220

B 232   **D** 158

3 Which group shows numbers in order from least to greatest?

A 32, 29, 46   **C** 85, 72, 51

B 18, 21, 62   **D** 44, 62, 57

4 Which group shows numbers in order from greatest to least?

A 763, 376, 373, 367

B 373, 367, 376, 763

C 367, 373, 763, 376

D 367, 373, 376, 763

5 The table shows the areas of different towns in New York State.

Town	Area in Square Miles
Albany	524
Geneseo	633
Ithaca	427
Waterloo	327

Which list names the towns from smallest to largest?

A Albany, Geneseo, Ithaca, Waterloo

B Geneseo, Albany, Ithaca, Waterloo

C Waterloo, Ithaca, Albany, Geneseo

D Waterloo, Ithaca, Geneseo, Albany

6 This picture shows the numbers of shells three friends collected at the seashore.

Frank   **Lisa**   **Marco**
75 shells   69 shells   57 shells

Which statement is true?

A Frank has fewer shells than Marco but more than Lisa.

B Lisa has more shells than Frank but fewer than Marco.

C Marco has fewer shells than Frank but more than Lisa.

D Lisa has more shells than Marco but fewer than Frank.

Read each problem. Write your answers.

7   Carlos collected four boxes of marbles. The first box had 213 marbles. The second box had 312 marbles. The third box had 132 marbles. The fourth box had 123 marbles.

Part A

Write the number of marbles in the boxes in order, from least to greatest.

Answer: _____123, 132, 213, 312_____

Part B

Explain how you found your answer.

First look at the digits in the hundreds places to find the smallest number. The numbers 123 and 132 both have a 1 in the hundreds place. Look at the digits in the tens places: 2 is smaller than 3. So the first two numbers are 123 and 132. The other two numbers are 213 and 312. Compare the hundreds digits: 2 is smaller than 3, so 213 is the next number. The number 312 is the largest.

8   Look at these number sentences.

189 ☐ 201   647 ☐ 674   959 ☐ 958

Part A

Write < or > in the boxes to make each number sentence true.

Part B

On the lines below, explain how you found each answer.

_____

_____

_____

_____

Read the problem. Write your answer for each part.

9 Sachiko loves baseball. The table shows the number of games her favorite teams have won so far this season.

Team	Wins
New York Yankees	27
New York Mets	25
Baltimore Orioles	30
Philadelphia Phillies	23

Part A

List the teams in order from greatest to least number of wins.

Answer: _____

_____

_____

Ask Yourself
Which place value should I look at first?

Part B

The Toronto Blue Jays have won 26 games. If this team were included, where would it go in the list you made for Part A?

Answer: _____

_____

Part C

Sachiko later updated her table. The Yankees won 2 more games, the Mets won 3 more games, the Orioles won 0 games, and the Phillies won 8 games. How will the order change?

_____

_____

_____

Unit 1 Whole Numbers and Fractions

25

Indicators 3.N.10, 11, 12, 13 **CCSS** 3.NF.1

✔ A **fraction** can name part of a whole.

$$\frac{1}{3}$$ one-third

To name a fraction, write the number of parts talked about as the **numerator.** Write the number of equal parts in the whole as the **denominator.**

one-third = $\frac{1}{3}$ ← Numerator
← Denominator

The circle has 1 shaded part. It has 3 equal parts in all. The fraction $\frac{1}{3}$ names the shaded part of the whole circle.

✔ A fraction can name part of a set.

There are 2 apples with worms in a set of 4 apples.

So $\frac{2}{4}$ of the apples have worms.

Remember—

The numerator and the denominator are the **terms** of the fraction.

$\frac{1}{8}$ ← Numerator
← Denominator

The parts of a fraction must be *equal* in size.

These are fourths.

These are *not* fourths.

A **unit fraction *always*** has 1 for a numerator. These are unit fractions:

One-half	$\frac{1}{2}$
One-third	$\frac{1}{3}$
One-fourth	$\frac{1}{4}$
One-fifth	$\frac{1}{5}$
One-sixth	$\frac{1}{6}$
One-eighth	$\frac{1}{8}$
One-tenth	$\frac{1}{10}$

Read each problem. Circle the letter of the best answer.

1 This picture shows a group of dogs.

What fraction of the group of dogs is spotted?

A $\frac{1}{2}$ C $\frac{1}{4}$

B $\frac{1}{3}$ D $\frac{1}{5}$

> The correct answer is D. There are 5 dogs in the group. Four of the dogs are a solid color. One dog is spotted. The fraction of the group that is spotted is $\frac{1}{5}$.

2 Which fraction has a numerator of 2 and a denominator of 3?

A $\frac{2}{5}$ C $\frac{2}{3}$

B $\frac{3}{2}$ D $\frac{1}{3}$

3 Which square has $\frac{1}{4}$ shaded?

A   C

B   D

4 Four pies were cut into different sizes. Which pie was cut into sixths?

A   C

B   D

5 Look at the set of cards below.

What fraction of the cards has triangles?

A $\frac{1}{4}$ C $\frac{1}{2}$

B $\frac{4}{1}$ D $\frac{2}{1}$

6 Eva was playing jacks. These jacks were on the ground.

Eva picked up $\frac{1}{3}$ of the jacks on her turn. How many jacks did she pick up?

A 1   C 5

B 2   D 6

7 Crystal planted beans in $\frac{1}{10}$ of her garden. How many parts was her garden divided into?

A 1   C 5

B 2   D 10

Read each problem. Write your answers.

8 This hexagon is divided into 6 equal parts.

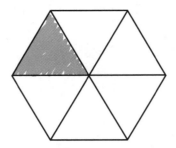

Part A

Shade $\frac{1}{6}$ of the figure above.

Part B

What fraction of the hexagon is **not** shaded? Explain.

> The hexagon has 6 equal parts. The fraction $\frac{1}{6}$ represents 1 out of 6. So 1 of the 6 parts should be shaded. There are 5 sections that are **not** shaded. So 5 of the 6 parts are not shaded, or $\frac{5}{6}$.

9 Benito had these pretzels. He ate $\frac{1}{2}$ of them.

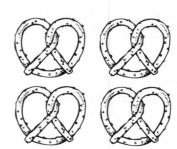

Part A

Circle the pretzels Benito ate. What fraction of the pretzels did Benito have left?

Answer: _____

Part B

Explain how you found your answer.

_____

_____

_____

_____

Unit 1 Whole Numbers and Fractions

Read the problem. Write your answer for each part.

10 Paul is mowing a lawn.

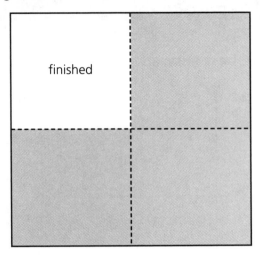

Part A

What fraction of the lawn did Paul finish?

Answer: _____

Part B

What fraction of the lawn does Paul have left to mow?

Answer: _____

Part C

Explain how you found your answer.

_____

_____

_____

_____

_____

_____

Ask Yourself
How many equal parts are on the lawn?

Whole Numbers and Fractions Review

Read each problem. Circle the letter of the best answer.

1 The Statue of Liberty is 151 feet tall. What is the word name for this number?

    A one hundred fifteen

    B one hundred fifty-one

    C one hundred fifty-five

    D one hundred eleven

2 What number does this picture show?

    A 81   **C** 118

    B 108   **D** 180

3 Which statement about skip counting is true?

    A If you are counting by 25's, the next number after 325 is 400.

    B If you are counting by 50's, the next number after 300 is 325.

    C If you are counting by 50's, the next number after 450 is 500.

    D If you are counting by 100's, the next number after 600 is 650.

4 A certain amount of money was raised for a food drive. The number has a 5 in the tens place. Which number could it be?

    A $579   **C** $795

    B $759   **D** $975

5 Which shows a way to make 375?

    A 300 + 50 + 50

    B 400 − 75

    C 300 + 65 + 10

    D 300 − 75

6 Which of the boxes shows fifths?

    A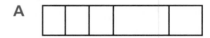

    B

    C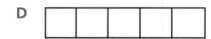

    D

7 Shonelle is counting by 25's. Which list names the three numbers she will say next after 475?

    A 500, 525, 550

    B 500, 550, 600

    C 500, 600, 700

    D 525, 575, 625

8 Which number sentence is true?

    A 812 > 821   **C** 648 > 684

    B 705 < 579   **D** 584 < 736

Read each problem. Write your answers.

9 In 1815, there were only 331 people living in Rochester, New York.

Part A

Write the word name of the number 331.

Answer: _____

Part B

Write this number in expanded form.

Answer: _____

10 The Erie Canal was built more than 175 years ago. This New York State landmark is 75 feet wide!

Part A

Use addition to show another way to make 175.

Answer: _____

Part B

Use subtraction to show another way to make 75.

Answer: _____

11 Mrs. Garcia bought these cans of juice.

Part A

What fraction of the cans is grape juice?

Answer: _____

Part B

Explain how you found your answer.

_____

_____

_____

Read the problem. Write your answer for each part.

12   Mike and Yolanda collect basketball cards. Each of them has a
     three-digit number of cards.

   Part A

   Mike's number has a 7 in the ones place, a 2 in the hundreds place,
   and a 0 in the tens place.

   How many cards does Mike have?

   Answer: _____ cards

   Part B

   Yolanda's number has a 6 in the tens place, a 3 in the ones place, and
   a 2 in the hundreds place.

   How many cards does Yolanda have?

   Answer: _____ cards

   Part C

   Who collected more cards?

   Answer: _____

   Explain how you know.

   _____

   _____

Unit 1 Whole Numbers and Fractions

Unit 2
Number Theory

Numbers have certain characteristics that are always true. All numbers are either even or odd. When you do operations with numbers, it helps to know the properties, or rules, of operations. This unit will help you to use the properties of numbers and operations.

Lesson 1 **Odd and Even Numbers** reviews how to decide if a number is even or odd. You will also review how to decide if a sum will be even or odd.

Lesson 2 **Properties of Addition** reviews the commutative and associative properties of addition.

Lesson 3 **Properties of Multiplication** reviews the commutative property of multiplication. You will also review the identity property and zero property.

✔ **Even numbers** end in 0, 2, 4, 6, or 8.

2, 1**2**, 3**0**, 5**6**, 7**4**, 9**8**

These are all even numbers.

○ ○ ○ ○

There is an even number of circles, 4.

✔ **Odd numbers** end in 1, 3, 5, 7, or 9.

5, 1**3**, 4**7**, 6**1**, 8**5**, 9**9**

These are all odd numbers.

△ △ △

There is an odd number of triangles, 3.

Every odd number is 1 more than an even number.

$$7 = 6 + 1$$

$$15 = 14 + 1$$

✔ When you add numbers, the sum will be even or odd depending on the addends.

When you add two even numbers, the sum is always even.

$$14 + 4 = 18$$

When you add two odd numbers, the sum is always even.

$$11 + 5 = 16$$

When you add an even number and an odd number, the sum is always odd.

$$8 + 5 = 13$$

Remember—

You say even numbers when you count by 2's: two, four, six, eight, ten, …

All even numbers can be divided evenly by 2.

The numbers you add are the **addends.** The result is the **sum.**

$$\begin{array}{r} 4 \leftarrow \text{Addend} \\ +5 \leftarrow \text{Addend} \\ \hline 9 \leftarrow \text{Sum} \end{array}$$

Subtraction is the inverse, or opposite, of addition.

$9 - 4 = 5$ because
$5 + 4 = 9$

Even − even = even
$10 - 6 = 4$

Odd − odd = even
$11 - 5 = 6$

Even − odd = odd
$12 - 5 = 7$

Odd − even = odd
$11 - 4 = 7$

Read each problem. Circle the letter of the best answer.

1 Which of these sums is an even number?

   A $9 + 2$

   B $7 + 3$

   C $2 + 5$

   D $4 + 7$

The correct answer is B. Choices A, C, and D are the sums of an even number and an odd number, which is always odd. The sum of two odd numbers is always even: $7 + 3 = 10$.

2 What are the odd numbers between 40 and 50?

   A 42, 44, 46, 48, 50

   B 41, 42, 44, 45, 47

   C 41, 43, 45, 47, 49

   D 42, 44, 46, 47, 49

3 Which of the following **best** describes the group of numbers below?

       21, 23, 35, 37, 39

   A None are even or odd.

   B They are all even.

   C They are all odd.

   D Some are even and some are odd.

4 Abby's age is an even number. Claire is 2 years younger. Which of these could be Claire's age?

   A 5

   B 6

   C 7

   D 9

5 Which group has an even number of circles?

   A O O O O O O O O O

   B O O O O O O O

   C O O O O O O O O O

   D O O O O O O O O O O O

6 Which set shows only odd numbers?

   A {61, 62, 63, 64, 65}

   B {51, 53, 55, 56, 58}

   C {34, 36, 38, 40, 42}

   D {43, 45, 47, 49, 51}

7 Which of these differences is an odd number?

   A $5 - 1$

   B $8 - 2$

   C $3 - 2$

   D $7 - 1$

Read each problem. Write your answers.

8   Mrs. Campbell collected math homework from 27 students. She collected science homework from 19 students.

Part A

Was the total number of homework papers she collected odd or even?

Answer: _____ *even* _____

Part B

Explain how you know your answer is correct.

> Odd numbers all end in 1, 3, 5, 7, or 9. The number of math papers, 27, ends in 7, so it is an odd number. The number of science papers, 19, ends in a 9, so it is also odd. The sum of an odd number and an odd number is always even: 27 + 19 = 46.

9   Use your counters to help you solve this problem.

Bob added two numbers and got a sum of 9.

Part A

Were the numbers he added even or odd?

Answer: _____

Part B

What two numbers could he have added?

Answer: _____ and _____

Read the problem. Write your answer for each part.

10 Mr. Rodriguez brought a box of oranges to school. He gave 2 oranges to each student. There was 1 orange left in the box.

Part A

Was the total number of oranges in the box odd or even?

Answer: _____

Ask Yourself
Did he give an even or odd number of oranges to each student?

Part B

Explain how you found your answer.

_____

_____

_____

_____

Part C

Was the total number Mr. Rodriguez gave to his students even or odd? Why?

_____

_____

_____

_____

_____

_____

Properties of Addition

Indicators   3.N.6, 9

✓ You can add numbers in any order and the sum will be the same. This is called the **commutative property.**

$$5 + 2 = 7 \qquad 2 + 5 = 7$$

So $5 + 2 = 2 + 5$.

✓ You can group numbers in any order to add. This is called the **associative property.**

$$(15 + 12) + 5 = 15 + (12 + 5)$$

$$27 + 5 = 15 + 17$$

$$32 = 32$$

Remember—

You **cannot** subtract numbers in any order.

$$7 - 5$$

is not the same as

$$5 - 7$$

Addition and subtraction are **inverse,** or opposite, operations.

Parentheses ( ) are grouping symbols. Always work inside parentheses first.

The associative property is **not** true for subtraction.

$$10 - (5 - 3) \neq (10 - 5) - 3$$
$$10 - 2 \neq 5 - 3$$
$$8 \neq 2$$

You can add 0 to a number. The number stays the same.

$$43 + 0 = 43 \qquad 0 + 15 = 15$$

When you subtract a number from itself, the difference is 0.

$$9 - 9 = 0$$

When you subtract 0 from a number, the difference is the number.

$$9 - 0 = 9$$

Read each problem. Circle the letter of the best answer.

1 Which expression gives the same answer as $(9 + 4) + 7$?

A $(9 + 4) \times 7$

B $(9 \times 4) + 7$

C $9 \times (4 \times 7)$

D $9 + (4 + 7)$

> The correct answer is D. The associative property says you can group numbers in any order to add. So $(9 + 4) + 7 = 9 + (4 + 7)$.

2 Which number makes this number sentence true?

$$6 + \square = 12 + 6$$

A 0

B 1

C 6

D 12

3 Which expression has the same sum as $6 + 9$?

A $9 + 6$

B $9 + 9$

C $9 + 0$

D $6 + 0$

4 What number goes in the box to make this number sentence true?

$$(\square + 12) + 9 = 8 + (12 + 9)$$

A 9

B 0

C 8

D 12

5 What number goes in the box to make this number sentence true?

$$\square + 12 = 12 + 5$$

A 0

B 5

C 12

D 17

6 Which expression gives the same answer as $(23 + 7) + 62$?

A $23 + (7 + 62)$

B $23 + (7 \times 62)$

C $(23 \times 7) \times 62$

D $(23 \times 7) + 62$

7 Which number sentence is **not** true?

A $26 + (15 + 3) = (26 + 15) + 3$

B $17 - 0 = 17$

C $17 + 26 = 26 + 17$

D $26 - 17 = 17 - 26$

Read each problem. Write your answers.

8 Cliff bought 3 apples and 5 oranges. Janice bought 5 oranges and 3 apples.

Part A

Who bought more pieces of fruit, Cliff or Janet?

Answer: <u>They bought the same number of pieces of fruit.</u>

Part B

Explain why your answer is correct.

Adding numbers in any order will not change the sum. So 5 + 3 is the same as 3 + 5. The sum of each is 8. This is the commutative property of addition.

9 Dave has 10 red balloons, 13 blue balloons, and 8 green balloons. Katie has 8 red balloons and 13 blue balloons. Katie wants the same total number of balloons as Dave.

Part A

How many green balloons does Katie need?

Answer: _____

Part B

Explain how you know your answer is correct.

_____

_____

_____

_____

Read the problem. Write your answer for each part.

10 Look at this number sentence.

$$(\square + 15) + 2 = 5 + (15 + 2)$$

Part A

What number goes in the box to make the number sentence true?

Ask Yourself
What are the numbers on either side of the equals sign?

Answer: _____

Part B

Explain how you found your answer.

_____

_____

_____

Part C

What is the value of each side of the number sentence? Use your answer for Part A for the value of the box.

Show your work.

Answer: _____

Indicators   3.N.6, 7, 8   **CCSS**   3.OA.5

✓ You can multiply numbers in any order. The product is the same. This is called the **commutative property.**

$2 \times 4 = 8$ $4 \times 2 = 8$

So $2 \times 4 = 4 \times 2$.

✓ You can multiply or divide a number by 1. The number stays the same. This is called the **identity property.**

$5 \times 1 = 5$ $8 \div 1 = 8$

✓ You can multiply a number by 0. The product will be 0. It does not matter what order the numbers are in. This is called the **zero property of multiplication.**

$19 \times 0 = 0$ $0 \times 5 = 0$

Remember—

The numbers you multiply are **factors.** The result is the **product.**

$4 \leftarrow$ Factor
$\underline{\times 3} \leftarrow$ Factor
$12 \leftarrow$ Product

Multiplication and division are inverse operations.

You *cannot* divide numbers in any order.

$8 \div 4$
is *not* the same as
$4 \div 8$

When you divide any number by itself, the quotient is 1.

$7 \div 7 = 1$

When you divide a number by 1, the quotient is the number.

$7 \div 1 = 7$

Read each problem. Circle the letter of the best answer.

1 Which number sentence describes both pictures?

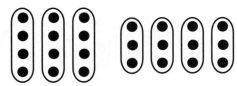

A   4 × 4 = 4 × 3

B   3 × 4 = 3 × 3

C   3 × 4 = 4 × 3

D   4 + 4 = 3 × 4

> The correct answer is C. You can multiply numbers in any order. The product is the same. Choice A is incorrect since 16 does not equal 12. Choice B is wrong because 12 does not equal 9, and choice D is wrong since 8 does not equal 12.

2 What number goes in the box to make this number sentence true?

$$8 \times \Box = 8$$

A   0   C   2

B   1   D   8

3 What statement is true about the missing number in each of these number sentences?

$$7 \times \Box = 0 \qquad \Box \times 19 = 0$$

A   It is always 1.

B   It is never 0.

C   It is always 0.

D   It is 7 or 19.

4 What number goes in the box to make this number sentence true?

$$8 \times 2 = \Box \times 8$$

A   2

B   4

C   10

D   16

5 Tyler has a number. When he multiplies it by 1, the product is 10. What is Tyler's number?

A   0

B   1

C   9

D   10

6 Which of these number sentences is true?

A   7 × 0 = 7

B   7 × 1 = 1

C   0 × 7 = 0

D   1 × 7 = 1

7 Janet had 5 boxes filled with 9 books in each box. Alan had an equal number of books in 9 boxes. How many books were in each of Alan's boxes?

A   4

B   5

C   9

D   14

Read each problem. Write your answers.

8 Look at the number sentence below.

$$13 \times \square = 13$$

Part A

What number completes this number sentence?

Answer: _____1_____

Part B

Explain why your answer is correct.

> The problem asks what number times another number results in the same number as the product. The identity property says you can multiply any number by 1 and the number will be the same. So $13 \times 1 = 13$.

9 Mr. Jones wrote this number sentence on the board.

$$21 \times \square = 0$$

Part A

What number goes in the box to make the number sentence true?

Answer: _____

Part B

Explain why your answer is correct.

_____

_____

_____

_____

Read the problem. Write your answer for each part.

10 There were 5 groups of 2 people talking in the park. There were 2 groups of 5 people talking in the playground.

Part A

Draw pictures to show this number sentence.

5 groups of 2 = 2 groups of 5

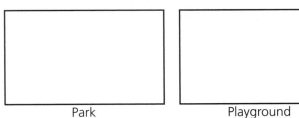

Park   Playground

> **Ask Yourself**
> How many groups are there? How many people are in each group?

Part B

Which place had the most people talking?

Answer: _____

Part C

Explain why your answer is correct.

_____

_____

_____

_____

Number Theory Review

Read each problem. Circle the letter of the best answer.

1 Which of these number sentences is true?

   A $12 \times 0 = 12$

   B $12 \times 1 = 1$

   C $0 \times 12 = 0$

   D $1 \times 12 = 1$

2 Which expression gives the same answer as $(5 + 2) + 4$?

   A $(5 + 5) + 2$ **C** $4 + (2 + 4)$

   B $5 + (2 + 4)$ **D** $(5 + 3) + 4$

3 Which number sentence describes both pictures?

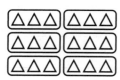

   A $6 \times 6 = 3 \times 6$

   B $3 + 6 = 6 \times 3$

   C $3 \times 6 = 3 \times 3$

   D $6 \times 3 = 3 \times 6$

4 Which set shows only odd numbers?

   A {31, 33, 41, 45, 51}

   B {30, 35, 37, 43, 50}

   C {29, 39, 42, 53, 59}

   D {28, 30, 36, 40, 46}

5 What number goes in the box to make this number sentence true?

$$7 + 8 = \square + 7$$

   A 1   **C** 15

   B 8   **D** 56

6 Which of these sums is an even number?

   A $5 + 2$

   B $6 + 7$

   C $8 + 5$

   D $9 + 3$

7 What is true about the missing number in each of these number sentences?

$$4 \times \square = 4 \qquad \square \times 17 = 17$$

   A It is always 0.

   B It is 4 or 17.

   C It is always 1.

   D It is never 1.

8 Which expression has the same sum as $8 + 15$?

   A $15 + 8$

   B $15 + 15$

   C $8 + 8$

   D $8 + 15 + 8$

Read each problem. Write your answers.

9 Jermaine ran a race in 19 seconds. Phil ran it in 14 seconds.

Part A

Was Jermaine's time an odd number or an even number?

Answer: _____

Part B

Is the difference between the times an odd number or an even number? Explain.

_____

_____

10 Look at this number sentence.

$$(\Box + 10) + 4 = 7 + (10 + 4)$$

Part A

What number goes in the box to make this number sentence true?

Answer: _____

Part B

Explain your answer.

_____

_____

11 Allison wrote the following number sentence on the board.

$$\Box \times 12 = 0$$

Part A

What number would complete this number sentence?

Answer: _____

Part B

What multiplication property does the number sentence show?

Answer: _____

Read the problem. Write your answer for each part.

12 At a summer camp, 7 boys slept in each of 6 cabins and 6 girls slept in each of 7 cabins.

Part A

Were there more boys or more girls at the camp?

Answer: _____

Part B

Explain why your answer is correct.

_____

_____

_____

Part C

During one afternoon, there were 5 campers boating and 3 campers swimming. The same number of campers were hiking and riding horses. There were 3 campers hiking. How many campers were riding horses?

Answer: _____ campers

Unit 3
Operations

Addition, subtraction, multiplication, and division are operations. There are certain steps you follow when you do these operations. Sometimes you must read a problem and decide which operation you should use. This unit will help you do these operations with whole numbers.

Lesson 1 **Adding Whole Numbers** reviews how to add two- and three-digit whole numbers.

Lesson 2 **Subtracting Whole Numbers** reviews how to subtract two- and three-digit whole numbers.

Lesson 3 **Multiplication Facts** reviews basic multiplication facts. You will also use arrays to show multiplication.

Lesson 4 **Division Facts** reviews basic division facts. You will use arrays to show division, too.

Lesson 5 **Multiplying Two-Digit Numbers** reviews how to multiply whole numbers.

Lesson 6 **Choosing the Operation** reviews how to decide what operation to use to find an answer.

Adding Whole Numbers

Indicator   3.N.18   CCSS   3.NBT.2

✓ Add numbers by adding the digits in the same places.

First add the ones.   Then add the tens.

$$\begin{array}{r} 23 \\ +15 \\ \hline 8 \end{array} \qquad \begin{array}{r} 23 \\ +15 \\ \hline 38 \end{array}$$

When the sum of two digits is 10 or more, **regroup.**

First add the ones and regroup.

$$\begin{array}{r} {\scriptstyle 1} \\ 58 \\ +16 \\ \hline 4 \end{array}$$ **8 + 6 = 14** ones, or **1** ten and **4** ones

Then add the tens.

$$\begin{array}{r} {\scriptstyle 1} \\ 58 \\ +16 \\ \hline 74 \end{array}$$ **1** ten + **5** tens + **1** ten = **7** tens

✓ Add numbers from right to left. If the sum of the digits in a place is 10 or more, regroup.

$$\begin{array}{r} {\scriptstyle 1} \\ 275 \\ +135 \\ \hline 0 \end{array}$$ First add the ones: 5 + 5 = 10 ones.
Regroup 10 ones as 1 ten.

$$\begin{array}{r} {\scriptstyle 11} \\ 275 \\ +135 \\ \hline 410 \end{array}$$ Next, add the tens: 1 + 7 + 3 = 11 tens.
Regroup 11 tens as 1 hundred and 1 ten.
Finally, add the hundreds: 1 + 2 + 1 = 4 hundreds.

Remember—

Add to combine numbers.

Addends are the numbers you add. The **sum** is the answer in an addition problem.

Addends
↓   ↓
7 + 3 = 10
↑
Sum

When you add, regroup from *right to left.*

Regroup 10 ones
as 1 ten.

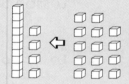

Read each problem. Circle the letter of the best answer.

1 Find the sum.

$$\begin{array}{r} 368 \\ +399 \\ \hline \end{array}$$

A 667   **C** 768

B 767   **D** 778

The correct answer is B. First add the ones: $8 + 9 = 17$. Regroup 17 ones as 1 ten and 7 ones. Next, add the tens: 1 ten + 6 tens + 9 tens = 16 tens. Regroup 16 tens as 1 hundred and 6 tens. Finally, add the hundreds: $1 + 3 + 3 = 7$.

$$\begin{array}{r} \overset{1\;1}{368} \\ +399 \\ \hline 767 \end{array}$$

2 There were 127 third graders at North Hills School, and 296 third graders at West Side Elementary School. How many third graders were there in all at these schools?

A 423   **C** 433

B 425   **D** 437

3 There were two trains at a station. There were 123 people on the first train. There were 129 people on the second train. How many people were on both trains?

A 242

B 244

C 251

D 252

4 Which number sentence is true?

A $648 + 175 = 823$

B $486 + 157 = 543$

C $684 + 175 = 759$

D $468 + 157 = 624$

5 Which addition problem needs regrouping?

A $526 + 373$

B $134 + 257$

C $845 + 143$

D $721 + 178$

6 Alaina read 138 books last year. Ravi read 143 books. How many books did they read altogether?

A 271

B 275

C 279

D 281

7 Find the sum.

$$\begin{array}{r} 228 \\ 167 \\ +249 \\ \hline \end{array}$$

A 533

B 543

C 644

D 654

Read each problem. Write your answers.

8 The Delgado family drove for three days to get to Niagara Falls, New York, for a vacation. Genny made this table. It shows how many miles her family drove each day.

Day	Miles Traveled
1	232
2	308
3	296

How many miles did the Delgados drive to get to Niagara Falls?

Show your work.

$$\begin{array}{r} \overset{1\ 1}{232} \\ 308 \\ +296 \\ \hline 836 \end{array}$$

Answer: ___836___ miles

First add the ones: $2 + 8 + 6 = 16$. Regroup as 1 ten and 6 ones. Then add the tens: $1 + 3 + 0 + 9 = 13$ tens. Regroup as 1 hundred and 3 tens. Finally, add the hundreds: $1 + 2 + 3 + 2 = 8$ hundreds.

9 The Clothes Rack had a sale on shirts, shorts, and sneakers. The table shows how much money was made on each item during the sale.

Item	Amount Made
Shirt	$180
Shorts	$202
Sneakers	$357

Part A

How much did the store make on shirts, shorts, and sneakers in all?

Show your work.

Answer: $_____

Part B

Explain why your answer is correct.

_____

_____

_____

Read the problem. Write your answer for each part.

10 This chart shows how high some places in a park are. The height of Eagle Point is the same as the heights of River Cliff and Big Hill together.

SUNSET PARK

Place	Height in Feet
River Cliff	591
Big Hill	115
Trail Overlook	436
Eagle Point	

Part A

How high is Eagle Point?

Show your work.

Ask Yourself
What is the height of River Cliff? What is the height of Big Hill?

Answer: _____ feet

Part B

Explain how you found your answer.

_____

_____

_____

_____

Indicator 3.N.18 CCSS 3.NBT.2

 Subtract numbers by subtracting the digits in the same places.

First subtract the ones.

$$\begin{array}{r} 79 \\ -25 \\ \hline 4 \end{array}$$

Then subtract the tens.

$$\begin{array}{r} 79 \\ -25 \\ \hline 54 \end{array}$$

When the digit in a place is not large enough to subtract from, regroup the next place to the left.

Regroup. Subtract the ones.

$$\begin{array}{r} \overset{5\ 10}{\cancel{6}\cancel{0}} \\ -13 \\ \hline 7 \end{array}$$
Regroup **6** tens as **5** tens and **10** ones.
10 ones − **3** ones = **7** ones

Subtract the tens.

$$\begin{array}{r} \overset{5\ 10}{\cancel{6}\cancel{0}} \\ -13 \\ \hline 47 \end{array}$$
5 tens − **1** ten = **4** tens

 Subtract numbers from right to left. If a digit is not large enough to subtract from, regroup the next place to the *left*.

$$\begin{array}{r} \overset{2\ 18}{2\cancel{3}\cancel{8}} \\ -129 \\ \hline 9 \end{array}$$
The digit in the ones place, 8, is less than 9, so regroup 3 tens as 2 tens and 10 ones. Now subtract the ones: 18 − 9 = 9 ones.

$$\begin{array}{r} \overset{2\ 18}{2\cancel{3}\cancel{8}} \\ -129 \\ \hline 109 \end{array}$$
Subtract the tens: 2 − 2 = 0 tens.
Subtract the hundreds: 2 − 1 = 1 hundred.

Remember—

Subtract to
- compare numbers
- find how many are left
- find a missing part

The **difference** is the answer to a subtraction problem.

$$\begin{array}{r} 228 \\ -\ 13 \\ \hline 215 \end{array} \leftarrow \text{Difference}$$

Addition and subtraction are *opposite* operations. You can add to check subtraction.

$$15 - 9 = 6$$
because
$$6 + 9 = 15$$

When you subtract, regroup from *left to right*.

Regroup 1 ten as 10 ones.

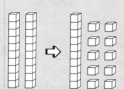

Read each problem. Circle the letter of the best answer.

1 One day, 175 children were at the park. If there were 147 boys, how many girls were at the park?

A   17

B   18

C   28

D   37

> The correct answer is C. To subtract 147 from 175, first regroup 7 tens as 6 tens and 10 ones. Subtract the ones, then the tens, and then the hundreds.
>
> $$\begin{array}{r} {}^{6\,15} \\ 17\!\!\!\not5 \\ -147 \\ \hline 28 \end{array}$$

2 Ian saved $250 to buy a new video game system. If he buys a system for $219, how much money will Ian have left?

A $31

B $35

C $41

D $44

3 A theater sold 500 movie tickets. If 270 tickets were for children, how many tickets were for adults?

A   130

B   230

C   330

D   770

4 Find the difference.

$$\begin{array}{r} 643 \\ -274 \\ \hline \end{array}$$

A   349

B   355

C   369

D   372

5 There were 300 people signed up to vote in the election. If 78 people did **not** vote, how many people voted?

A   212

B   222

C   232

D   278

6 Mr. Geller weighs 162 pounds, and Mrs. Geller weighs 138 pounds. What is the difference in their weights?

A   4 pounds

B   8 pounds

C   14 pounds

D   24 pounds

7 Find the difference.

$$\begin{array}{r} 713 \\ -369 \\ \hline \end{array}$$

A   334

B   344

C   347

D   352

Read each problem. Write your answers.

8 Kay lives 177 miles from Faith. Kay is taking a bus to Faith's house. The bus has traveled 19 miles.

How many miles does Kay still have to go?

Show your work.

$$
\begin{array}{r}
\overset{6}{\cancel{1}}\overset{17}{\cancel{7}}7 \\
-\ \ 19 \\
\hline
158
\end{array}
$$

Answer: ____158____ miles

> To subtract 19 from 177, first line up the numbers. You can't subtract 9 ones from 7 ones, so regroup 7 tens as 6 tens and 10 ones. There are $10 + 7 = 17$ ones in all. Then subtract the ones: $17 - 9 = 8$ ones. Then subtract the tens: $6 - 1 = 5$ tens. Then subtract the hundreds: $1 - 0 = 1$ hundred.

9 The Melendez family bought a swing set for $219. They saw the same swing set on sale for $189.

Part A

How much less did the sale swing set cost than the one the Melendez family bought?

Show your work.

Answer: $_____

Part B

Explain how you found your answer.

_____

_____

_____

_____

Read the problem. Write your answer for each part.

10 This table shows the prices for some flat-panel televisions.

Brand	Price
GI	$379
RBA	$445
Sonic	$560

Part A

What is the difference in price between the most expensive TV and the least expensive TV?

Show your work.

Ask Yourself
Which TV costs the most? Which TV costs the least?

Answer: $_____

Part B

Explain why your answer is correct.

_____

_____

_____

_____

Multiplication Facts

Indicators 3.N.19, 21 **CCSS** 3.OA.1, 3, 4, 5

✔ **Multiply** to combine groups of equal size.

The store sold 6 bags of goldfish. Each bag held 5 goldfish. How many goldfish did the store sell in all?

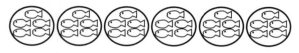

$6 \times 5 = 30$ goldfish

$5 + 5 + 5 + 5 + 5 + 5 = 30$ goldfish

6 groups of 5 = 30 goldfish

$$\begin{array}{r} 5 \\ \times 6 \\ \hline 30 \text{ goldfish} \end{array}$$

✔ You can use an **array** or other model to show multiplication.

Hassam, Jeff, and Ina ate 4 pretzels each. How many pretzels did the children eat in all?

This array shows 3 rows of 4.

● ● ● ●
● ● ● ●
● ● ● ●

$4 + 4 + 4 = 3$ rows of 4

$3 \times 4 = 12$

$$\begin{array}{r} 4 \\ \times 3 \\ \hline 12 \end{array}$$

The children ate 12 pretzels in all.

Remember—

Factors are the numbers you multiply to get a **product.**

$$\begin{array}{r} 4 \leftarrow \text{Factor} \\ \times 3 \leftarrow \text{Factor} \\ \hline 12 \leftarrow \text{Product} \end{array}$$

Factor   Product
↓   ↓
$3 \times 4 = 12$
↑
Factor

You can multiply numbers in any order. This is called the commutative property.

$9 \times 3 = 27$ $3 \times 9 = 27$

You can multiply a number by 1 and the number stays the same.

$8 \times 1 = 8$ $1 \times 13 = 13$

You can multiply a number by 0 and the product will be 0.

$5 \times 0 = 0$ $0 \times 16 = 0$

Read each problem. Circle the letter of the best answer.

1 Haroun set 5 plates on the table. He placed 3 cookies on each plate. How many cookies did Haroun put on the plates in all?

A   8

B   15

C   18

D   35

The correct answer is B. To combine groups of equal size, multiply: 5 × 3 = 15. Choice A gives the sum of the numbers. Choices C and D do not make sense.

2 Mrs. Brandt bought 6 packs of hot dogs.

How many hot dogs did Mrs. Brandt buy in all?

A   14   C   48

B   42   D   68

3 Which number sentence shows the array below?

A $4 \times 4 = \square$

B $5 \times 5 = \square$

C $5 \times 3 = \square$

D $4 \times 5 = \square$

4 Four children went to the movies on Saturday. Each ticket cost $6. How much did the children spend in all on tickets?

A $2   C $24

B $10   D $30

5 Seven students each borrowed 9 books from the library. Which number sentence could you solve to find the total number of books they borrowed?

A $7 + 9 = \square$ C $7 \times 9 = \square$

B $9 - 7 = \square$ D $9 \div 7 = \square$

6 Find the product.

$$8 \times 2 = \square$$

A   6   C   16

B   10   D   24

7 Which model shows 3 × 7?

Read each problem. Write your answers.

8 Nine cars are waiting at a car wash. It takes 6 minutes for one car to go through the car wash.

Part A

How long will it take for all the cars to go through the car wash?

Answer: _____54_____ minutes

Part B

Explain how you found your answer.

> You are asked to find the total time it takes to wash a number of cars. Multiply the number of cars times the number of minutes it takes to wash each car: 9×6 minutes = 54 minutes.

9 There are 8 cans of tennis balls. There are 3 tennis balls in each can.

Part A

How many tennis balls are in the cans in all? Draw a picture to show this problem.

Answer: _____ tennis balls

Part B

Explain why your answer is correct.

_____

_____

_____

_____

Read the problem. Write your answer for each part.

10 Adam bought 5 stickers for 9¢ each. Sydney bought 9 stickers for 5¢ each.

Part A

Who spent more money, Adam or Sydney?

Show your work.

Ask Yourself
What operation would you use to find how much each person spent?

Answer: _____

Part B

Explain why your answer is correct.

_____

_____

_____

_____

_____

_____

Division Facts

Indicators   3.N.22, 23   **CCSS**   3.OA.2, 3, 6

✅ **Divide** to break a group into groups of equal size.

The store has 28 guppies. There are 4 tanks with the same number of guppies in each. How many guppies are in each tank?

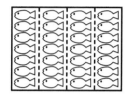

$$28 \div 4 = 7 \text{ guppies}$$

$$\begin{array}{r} 7 \\ 4\overline{)28} \\ \underline{28} \end{array}$$

There are 7 guppies in each tank.

✅ You can use an **array** or other model to show division.

A package of cookie dough makes 24 cookies. If the 6 members of the Roberts family share the cookies equally, how many cookies will each person get?

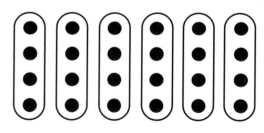

$$24 \div 6 = 4$$

$$\begin{array}{r} 4 \\ 6\overline{)24} \end{array}$$

Each person will get 4 cookies.

Remember—

The **dividend** is the number being divided. The **divisor** is the number doing the dividing. The **quotient** is the answer.

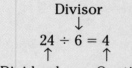

$$24 \div 6 = 4$$

Dividend Quotient

Quotient
↓
$$\begin{array}{r} 4 \\ \text{Divisor} \rightarrow 6\overline{)24} \\ \uparrow \\ \text{Dividend} \end{array}$$

Another way to show division is with a fraction.

$$\frac{12}{3} = 4$$

means the same as

$$12 \div 3 = 4$$

Multiplication and division are opposite operations. You can multiply to check division.

$$28 \div 4 = 7$$
because
$$7 \times 4 = 28$$

The word ***halve*** means "to divide by 2."

Unit 3 Operations

Read each problem. Circle the letter of the best answer.

1 Two friends shared a box of candy that had 16 ounces. Each friend ate the same amount. Which number sentence shows how many ounces each friend ate?

A $16 + 2 = 18$

B $16 - 2 = 14$

C $16 \times 2 = 32$

D $16 \div 2 = 8$

The correct answer is D. The problem asks you to break 16 ounces of candy into two equal parts for 2 friends. Division is the only operation that allows you to do this. Choices A and C combine two groups. Choice B shows what is left when 2 is taken away.

2 A teacher put 24 desks into 3 equal rows. Which number sentence would tell how many desks were in each row?

A $24 - 3 = \square$ **C** $24 \div 3 = \square$

B $3 \times 24 = \square$ **D** $3 \div 24 = \square$

3 Which picture is the **best** model of the division fact $15 \div 3 = 5$?

A

B

C

D

4 Nita and Hector planted 42 seeds in 6 equal rows. What number sentence could you solve to find how many seeds they planted in each row?

A $42 + 6 = \square$ **C** $42 \div 6 = \square$

B $42 \times 6 = \square$ **D** $42 - 6 = \square$

5 Divide.

$$12 \div 2 = \square$$

A 6   **C** 14

B 10   **D** 24

6 Mrs. Langer planted 21 peach trees in 3 equal rows.

Which number sentence would tell the number of trees in each row?

A $21 \div 3 = \square$ **C** $21 - 3 = \square$

B $21 \times 3 = \square$ **D** $21 + 3 = \square$

7 What rule does this table show?

12	6
10	5
8	4
6	3

A subtract 6   **C** multiply by 2

B add 6   **D** divide by 2

Read each problem. Write your answers.

8 Mariel has 3 dogs. She has 27 dog treats. She wants to give each dog the same number of treats.

Part A

How many treats will each dog get?

Answer: _____9_____ treats

Part B

Explain how you found your answer.

> The problem asks you to break the 27 dog treats into equal groups for the 3 dogs. Divide to find the answer: 27 ÷ 3 = 9. Each dog will get 9 treats.

9 A farmer put 81 apples into 9 bags. Each bag had the same number of apples.

Part A

Write a number sentence you could use to find out how many apples were in each bag.

Answer: _____

Part B

Explain why your answer is correct.

_____

_____

_____

_____

Read the problem. Write your answer for each part.

10 Caleb made this design.

Part A

Write two multiplication facts to match Caleb's design.

Answer 1: _____

Answer 2: _____

Ask Yourself
How many rows of pennies are there? How many pennies are in each row?

Part B

Write two division facts to match Caleb's design.

Answer 1: _____

Answer 2: _____

Part C

Explain how you found your answers.

_____

_____

_____

Indicators 3.N.20, 21 **CCSS** 3.OA.2, 3, 7

✓ Multiply whole numbers from right to left. Multiply the ones. Then multiply the tens.

A DVD cost $12. Louisa bought 6 of them. How much did she spend?

$$\begin{array}{r} 1 \\ \$12 \\ \times 6 \\ \hline \$72 \end{array}$$

Multiply the ones: $6 \times 2 = 12$ ones. Write the 2 in the ones place.

Regroup 10 ones as 1 ten and write it above the tens place.

Multiply the tens: $6 \times 1 = 6$ tens. Add the 1 ten for 7 tens. Write them in the product.

Louisa spent $72 on DVDs.

✓ To multiply by a two-digit number, first multiply by the ones to find a partial product. Then multiply by the tens to find a second partial product. Add the partial products.

A ticket to the laser show costs $11. A group of 12 people went to the show on Saturday. How much were their tickets?

$$\begin{array}{r} \$11 \\ \times 12 \\ \hline 22 \\ 110 \\ \hline \$132 \end{array}$$

Think of 12 as 1 ten and 2 ones.

Multiply by the ones: $2 \times 11 = 2 + 20 = 22$.

Multiply by the tens: $10 \times 11 = 10 + 100 = 110$.

Add the partial products: $22 + 110 = 132$.

The tickets for the group cost $132.

Remember—

You can use visual models to show multiplication and division.

• array

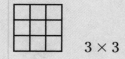

$2 \times 3 = 6$

$6 \div 2 = 3$

• area model

3×3

• patterns/rules

2, 4, 6, 8 "multiply by 2"

12, 6, 3 "divide by 2"

The word **double** means "to multiply by 2."

Read each problem. Circle the letter of the best answer.

1 Look at this area model.

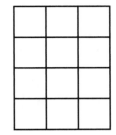

What number sentence shows this model?

A   4 ÷ 3

B   3 ÷ 12

C   4 × 3

D   12 × 3

The correct answer is C. The model shows
4 rows of 3 units. There are 12 units in all,
and 4 × 3 = 12.

2 There were 12 vans full of people visiting
Wild Water Park. Each van carried 8 people.
How many people were there altogether?

A   20

B   74

C   86

D   96

3 Thomas has 10 toy cars. Alec has double
the number of cars as Thomas. How many
cars does Alec have?

A   20

B   15

C   10

D   5

4 Find the product.

$$\begin{array}{r} 11 \\ \times 5 \\ \hline \end{array}$$

A   6

B   12

C   16

D   55

5 What does this model show?

OOOOOOOOOOO
OOOOOOOOOOO
OOOOOOOOOOO
OOOOOOOOOOO

A   11 ÷ 4

B   44 ÷ 4

C   4 × 11

D   44 × 4

6 What rule does this pattern show?

1, 3, 9, 27

A   multiply by 2

B   divide by 3

C   multiply by 3

D   divide by 2

Unit 3 Operations

67

Read each problem. Write your answers.

7   There are 11 floors of a building. Each floor has 11 windows.

How many windows are in the building in all?

Show your work.

$$\begin{array}{r} 11 \\ \times 11 \\ \hline 11 \\ 110 \\ \hline 121 \end{array}$$

Answer: _____121_____ windows

> There are 11 floors with 11 windows on each floor. Multiply to find how many windows in all. First multiply by the ones: $1 \times 11 = 11$ ones. Then multiply by the tens: $10 \times 11 = 110$. Then add the partial products: $11 + 110 = 121$. There are 121 windows in the whole building.

8   Shawn has 12 sheets of paper. He folds and tears each sheet into 6 pieces.

Part A

How many pieces of paper does he have now?

Show your work.

Answer: _____ pieces of paper

Part B

Explain how you know your answer is correct.

_____

_____

_____

Read the problem. Write your answer for each part.

9 A farmer wants to plant 11 rows of corn, with 12 plants in each row.

Part A

How many corn plants is the farmer planning to plant?

Show your work.

Answer: _____ plants

Part B

In the space below, draw an array to show how the farmer will plant the corn.

> *Ask Yourself*
> How many rows of corn will there be? How many columns?

Choosing the Operation

Indicator 3.N.24

✔ To solve problems, it is important to know which **operation** to choose.

Cliff collected 57 cans for recycling last week. This week, he collected 46 cans. How many cans did Cliff collect in all?

$$\begin{array}{r} 1 \\ 57 \\ +46 \\ \hline 103 \end{array}$$

Add the number of cans collected each week.

He collected 103 cans in all.

There were 85 people at the play on Friday and 93 people at the play on Saturday. How many more people were at the play on Saturday?

$$\begin{array}{r} 813 \\ \cancel{93} \\ -85 \\ \hline 8 \end{array}$$

Subtract the number of people on Friday from the number on Saturday.

There were 8 more people at the play on Saturday.

Marisol put her books on 4 shelves in her bedroom. Each shelf holds 8 books. How many books are on the shelves?

$$\begin{array}{r} 4 \\ \times 8 \\ \hline 32 \end{array}$$

Multiply the number of shelves by the number of books.

There are 32 books on the shelves.

In 5 days, 30 students signed up for the music program. The same number of students signed up each day. How many students joined the program each day?

$$\begin{array}{r} 6 \\ 5\overline{)30} \\ \underline{30} \end{array}$$

Divide the number of students by the number of days.

6 students signed up each day.

Remember—

Add to combine groups.

$$\begin{array}{r} 34 \leftarrow \text{Addend} \\ +17 \leftarrow \text{Addend} \\ \hline 51 \leftarrow \text{Sum} \end{array}$$

Subtract to

• compare numbers

• find how many are left

• find a missing part

$$\begin{array}{r} 200 \leftarrow \text{Minuend} \\ -13 \leftarrow \text{Subtrahend} \\ \hline 187 \leftarrow \text{Difference} \end{array}$$

Multiply to combine groups of equal size.

Six friends paid $3 each to go to the dance. How much money did they pay in all?

$$\begin{array}{r} \$3 \leftarrow \text{Factor} \\ \times 6 \leftarrow \text{Factor} \\ \hline \$18 \leftarrow \text{Product} \end{array}$$

Divide to break a group into groups of equal size.

Mom made 16 pancakes. She gave each of her children 4 pancakes. How many children does she have?

Dividend
↓
$16 \div 4 = 4 \leftarrow$ Quotient
↑
Divisor

Read each problem. Circle the letter of the best answer.

1 Alexandra had 40 CDs. She sorted them into 5 equal stacks. Which operation would you use to find how many CDs were in each stack?

  A division

  B addition

  C multiplication

  D subtraction

> The correct answer is A. The CDs are being split into 5 equal groups. To find the answer, divide: 40 ÷ 5 = 8. There were 8 CDs in each stack.

2 Mitchell is reading a book for his report. He reads 2 pages per minute. Which number sentence could you use to find how many pages Mitchell will read in 10 minutes?

  A $10 + 2 = \square$

  B $10 - 2 = \square$

  C $10 \div 2 = \square$

  D $10 \times 2 = \square$

3 Gloria scored 7 points higher than Herb on the last math test. Herb scored 70. What operation would you use to find Gloria's score?

  A division

  B multiplication

  C addition

  D subtraction

4 There were 65 people on a bus. When it stopped, 32 people got off the bus. Which number sentence would you use to find how many people were still on the bus?

  A $65 + 32 = \square$

  B $65 - 32 = \square$

  C $65 \times 32 = \square$

  D $65 \div 32 = \square$

5 Frey's Market sold 132 pints of strawberries last season. This season, they sold 172 pints. Which operation would you use to find how many pints of strawberries were sold in both seasons?

  A multiplication   **C** subtraction

  B addition   **D** division

6 Guy, Tayib, and Lane dug up 27 clams. The boys shared the clams equally. Which operation would you use to find how many clams each boy got?

  A addition   **C** multiplication

  B subtraction   **D** division

7 A clerk put 10 cans of soup on each of 6 shelves in a store. What number sentence would you use to find how many cans the clerk put on the shelves in all?

  A $10 \div 6 = \square$

  B $10 \times 6 = \square$

  C $10 - 6 = \square$

  D $10 + 6 = \square$

Read each problem. Write your answers.

8 Harding School is having a bake sale to raise money for the library.

Part A

Leon baked 9 bags of chocolate chip cookies. There are 8 cookies in each bag. Write a number sentence you could use to find how many chocolate chip cookies Leon baked.

Answer: _____ $9 \times 8 = 72$ _____

Part B

Explain why you chose that operation.

> There were 9 bags. Each bag had the same number of cookies, 8. Multiplication is used to combine groups of equal size. So you should multiply: $9 \times 8 = 72$ cookies.

9 A new football stadium was built in town.

Part A

Section 1 had 7 rows of seats. Each row had 10 seats. Section 2 had 8 rows with 8 seats in each row. What operation would you use to find how many seats were in each section?

Answer: _____

Part B

What operations would you use to compare the number of seats in the sections? Explain your answer.

_____

_____

_____

Read the problem. Write your answer for each part.

10 Mrs. Cavelli wrote these statements on the board:

1. 9 boxes with 18 books in each
2. 9 books in one pile and 18 books in another
3. 18 books and then 9 were read
4. 18 books put into 9 equal piles

Part A

Which operation does each statement represent?

Statement 1: _____

Statement 2: _____

Statement 3: _____

Statement 4: _____

> *Ask Yourself*
> What operation do
> I use to find each
> answer?

Part B

Which statement would result in the greatest number of books?

Show your work.

Statement: _____

Part C

Explain why your answer to Part B is correct.

_____

_____

_____

_____

Operations Review

Read each problem. Circle the letter of the best answer.

1 Which expression shows the model below?

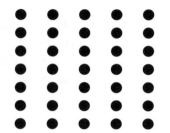

A 5 × 5

B 7 × 7

C 7 × 5

D 6 × 8

2 Which number sentence is **not** true?

A 382 + 79 = 461

B 594 + 28 = 874

C 837 + 55 = 892

D 869 + 36 = 905

3 Roberto copied 32 math problems on 8 pages in his notebook. He wrote an equal number of math problems on each page. Which number sentence could be used to find how many problems he wrote on each page?

A 32 × 8 = ☐

B 32 − 8 = ☐

C 8 + 32 = ☐

D 32 ÷ 8 = ☐

4 Emma has 3 packages of pens.

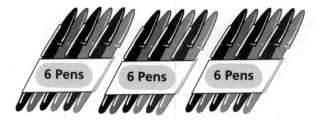

How many pens does Emma have?

A 12   **C** 18

B 15   **D** 24

5 Sammy gave 9 of his friends 12 stickers each. How many stickers did he give away?

A 3   **C** 101

B 21   **D** 108

6 Which picture is the **best** model of the division fact 10 ÷ 2?

A

B

C

D

7 Divide 81 ÷ 9.

A 9   **C** 72

B 27   **D** 90

Read each problem. Write your answers.

8 Troy and his father caught 12 sea trout. Each fish weighed an average of 3 pounds. What was the total weight of all the fish?

Show your work.

Answer: _____ pounds

9 For a field trip, 182 third graders and 191 fourth graders visited the zoo.

How many students in all visited the zoo?

Show your work.

Answer: _____ students

10 Tonya earned $48. She earned $6 per hour helping her grandmother.

Part A

Write a number sentence you would use to show how many hours Tonya worked to earn $48.

Answer: _____

Part B

Explain why you chose that operation.

_____

_____

_____

Read the problem. Write your answer for each part.

11   This picture shows how chairs were arranged for a poetry reading.

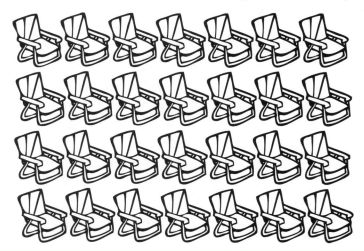

Part A

What multiplication fact does the picture show?

Answer: _____

Part B

Explain why your answer to Part A is correct.

_____

_____

_____

_____

Part C

What division fact could you use to find the number of chairs in each row?

Answer: _____

Unit 4
Estimation

Sometimes you do not need to find an exact answer. You can find an estimate. An estimate is a good guess. Use rounded numbers to help you estimate. This unit helps you round numbers and find good estimates.

Lesson 1 **Rounding** reviews how to round numbers to the nearest ten or hundred.

Lesson 2 **Estimating** reviews how to find a good estimate. You will also decide if an estimate is reasonable.

Rounding

Indicator   3.N.25   CCSS   3.NBT.1

✓ To **round** a whole number to a particular place, look at the digit in the **next** place to the right. If it is 4 or less, round down. If it is 5 or greater, round up.

✓ To round a number to the nearest ten, look at the ones.

What is 42 to the nearest ten?

Look at the ones:

↓
4**2**

2 is less than 5, so round down to 40.

What is 178 rounded to the nearest ten?

Look at the ones:

↓
17**8**

8 is greater than 5, so round up to 180.

✓ To round a number to the nearest hundred, look at the tens.

What is 438 rounded to the nearest hundred?

Look at the tens:

↓
4**3**8

3 is less than 5, so round down to 400.

What is 459 rounded to the nearest hundred?

Look at the tens:

↓
4**5**9

5 is equal to 5, so round up to 500.

Remember—

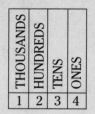

THOUSANDS	HUNDREDS	TENS	ONES
1	2	3	4

If the digit is—

0 1 2 3 4   5 6 7 8 9

←———   ———→
round   round
down   up

When you round a number, replace any digit **below** the place you are rounding to with a zero.

132

130 → to the nearest ten, use a zero for the ones place

100 → to the nearest hundred, use zeros for the tens and ones places

---

Unit 4 Estimation

Read each problem. Circle the letter of the best answer.

1 Which of these numbers rounds to 300?

A 221

B 235

C 344

D 362

The correct answer is C. To round to the nearest hundred, look at the digit in the tens place. It is a 4. So round 344 down to 300. Choices A and B round down to 200. Choice D rounds up to 400.

2 Which number would **not** round to 200?

A 138

B 163

C 236

D 245

3 Antoine read a 375-page book. When rounded to the nearest ten, how many pages did Antoine read?

A 300

B 360

C 370

D 380

4 Which statement is true when rounding to the nearest hundred?

A 171 becomes 100.

B 154 becomes 200.

C 235 becomes 300.

D 382 becomes 380.

5 There are 127 students in the third grade. What is this number rounded to the nearest ten?

A 100

B 120

C 130

D 140

6 When a number is rounded to the nearest ten, it is 350. When it is rounded to the nearest hundred, it is 300. What is the number?

A 329

B 346

C 359

D 366

7 What is 432 rounded to the nearest ten?

A 400

B 430

C 440

D 500

8 There were 274 people at a park over the weekend. What is this number rounded to the nearest ten?

A 300

B 280

C 275

D 270

Read each problem. Write your answers.

9 Mr. Perry wrote these numbers on the board:

197   289   321   348   359   419

Part A

Paul rounded the numbers to the nearest hundred. Which numbers rounded to 400?

Answer: ____359____ and ____419____

Part B

Explain your answer.

> To round to the nearest hundred, look at the digit in the tens place. If it is 4 or lower, round down. The numbers 321, 348, and 419 round down. But only 419 rounds down to 400. If it is 5 or higher, round up. The numbers 197, 289, and 359 round up. But only 359 rounds up to 400.

10 Graciella went bowling. Her score was 137.

Part A

What is Graciella's score rounded to the nearest ten?

Answer: _____

Part B

Omar's score also rounded to the same number as Graciella's score. What could his score have been? Name all the possible numbers.

Answer: _____

Read the problem. Write your answer for each part.

11 The Persaud family is driving to Buffalo to visit family. The distance
is 291 miles.

Part A

What is this distance rounded to the nearest ten miles?

Answer: _____ miles

Part B

What is this distance rounded to the nearest hundred miles?

Answer: _____ miles

Part C

The Gamble family drove a different distance to visit family. The
distance they drove can be rounded to the same numbers as the
distance the Persaud family drove. What are the distances the Gamble
family could have driven?

Answer: _____ miles

> **Ask Yourself**
> Is the digit in the
> ones place less than
> 5, or 5 or more?

Estimating

Indicators   3.N.26, 27   **CCSS**   3.OA.8

✓ To **estimate** a **sum,** first round the numbers. Then add.

There are 132 sheets of paper in a desk drawer and 108 sheets of paper on top of the desk. **About** how many sheets of paper are there?

Round to the nearest ten.

$$132 \text{ rounds to } 130$$
$$+108 \text{ rounds to } 110$$
$$\textbf{about } 240$$

There are **about** 240 sheets of paper.

✓ To **estimate** a **difference,** first round the numbers. Then subtract.

There are 395 sheets of paper in a box. Then Miguel uses 197 of the sheets to print a flyer. **About** how many sheets of paper are left in the box?

Round to the nearest hundred.

$$395 \text{ rounds to } 400$$
$$-197 \text{ rounds to } 200$$
$$\textbf{about } 200$$

There are **about** 200 sheets of paper left in the box.

✓ Use estimation to decide if an answer is reasonable.

There were 72 paper clips in a box. Then Erica used 16 paper clips. She believes there are 64 paper clips left. Is Erica's answer reasonable?

72 rounds down to 70 and 16 rounds up to 20. Subtract using the rounded numbers: $70 - 20 = 50$. So, no, 64 paper clips is **not** a reasonable answer. The actual answer would be closer to 50.

Remember—

To **round** a number to a certain place, look at the digit in the next place to the right.

If the digit is 1, 2, 3, or 4, round **down.**

34 rounds down to 30.

93 rounds down to 90.

If the digit is 5, 6, 7, 8, or 9, round **up.**

36 rounds up to 40.

98 rounds up to 100.

You can round numbers to the nearest ten or the nearest hundred, depending on how accurate the estimate must be.

Unit 4 Estimation

Read each problem. Circle the letter of the best answer.

1 Which of these statements is **most likely** an estimate?

A   The CD cost $14.99.

B   The class has 27 students.

C   There were 100 people at the game.

D   The Browns have 4 children.

The correct answer is C. It is easy to count the number of students in a class and the number of children in a family. The price $14.99 is probably shown on the CD. The number of people at a game is most likely an estimate.

2 Cooper scored 18 points in Tuesday's game, 24 points in Thursday's game, and 29 points in Saturday's game. He estimates that he scored about 80 points in the three games. Is his estimate reasonable?

A   Yes, he scored **about** 80 points.

B   No, he scored **about** 60 points.

C   No, he scored **about** 70 points.

D   No, he scored **about** 90 points.

3 A mountain bike sells for $298. It is on sale for $229. Jeremy estimates he will save about $70 buying it on sale. Is his estimate reasonable?

A   Yes, he will save **about** $70.

B   No, he will save **about** $60.

C   No, he will save **about** $80.

D   No, he will save **about** $100.

4 Which of these statements is **most likely** an estimate?

A   The distance from New York City to Rochester is 300 miles.

B   There are 10 windows in the house.

C   There are 24 crayons in a box.

D   The new TV cost $229.

5 There were 87 people at the skating rink on Friday and 114 people there on Saturday. Fran thinks there were about 180 people at the rink. Is her estimate reasonable?

A   Yes, the answer should be **about** 180.

B   No, the answer should be **about** 190.

C   No, the answer should be **about** 200.

D   No, the answer should be **about** 210.

6 Which of these statements is **most likely** an estimate?

A   There are 30 days in September.

B   The movie ticket cost $9.00.

C   There are 250 spaces in the parking lot.

D   Mr. Laurel works 40 hours per week.

7 Neil earned $27 last month. He spent $14 on movies. Which is the **most** reasonable estimate of the money Neil has left?

A   between $5 and $10

B   between $10 and $15

C   between $15 and $20

D   between $20 and $25

Read each problem. Write your answers.

8 Mr. Abraham ordered 200 programs for next Friday's football game.

   Part A

   Did Mr. Abraham **most likely** use estimation to get the total number of programs?

   Answer: _____ yes _____

   Part B

   Explain how you know.

   > It is difficult to get an exact count of the number of people at a football game before the game. Mr. Abraham probably knew about how many people come to the games. So he was able to estimate the number of programs needed. There may be a few more or a few less programs needed.

9 Mrs. Kennedy drove 38 miles to work and 42 miles home from work. She estimated that she drove 80 miles to and from work.

   Part A

   Is her estimate reasonable?

   Answer: _____

   Part B

   Explain why your answer is correct.

   _____

   _____

   _____

Read the problem. Write your answer for each part.

10 LaShawn bought a sweatshirt for $29, a pair of jeans for $33, and a hat for $17. He figured the total bill would be about $63.

Part A

Is LaShawn's answer reasonable?

Answer: _____

Ask Yourself About how much is each item?

Part B

Use estimation to explain why or why not.

_____

_____

_____

_____

Part C

How would you estimate the amount of change LaShawn would get from $100?

_____

_____

_____

Read each problem. Circle the letter of the best answer.

1 Tina collected 328 pennies. How many pennies did Tina collect rounded to the nearest ten?

   A 300   **C** 330

   B 320   **D** 400

2 Which of these statements is **most likely** an estimate?

   A There are 16 players on the team.

   B Jason scored 32 points in the game.

   C There were 500 people at the fair.

   D The store sold 46 fruit baskets.

3 Alex was planning a party. He spent $85 on food, $32 on decorations, and $26 for music. He figures that he spent about $130. Is his estimate reasonable?

   A Yes, he spent **about** $130.

   B No, he spent **about** $100.

   C No, he spent **about** $150.

   D No, he spent **about** $180.

4 When a number is rounded to the nearest hundred, it is 200. When it is rounded to the nearest ten, it is 240. What could be the number?

   A 237   **C** 250

   B 246   **D** 253

5 A beginner violin sells for $114. It is on sale for $76. Which is the **most** reasonable estimate of the amount of savings?

   A between $25 and $30

   B between $30 and $35

   C between $35 and $40

   D between $40 and $45

6 In which example would you **most likely** give an estimate?

   A the number of inches in a foot

   B the number of people at a party

   C the number of days in a week

   D the cost of a video game

7 A truck driver drove 312 miles one day and 281 miles the next day. He estimates that he drove about 600 miles in the two days. Is his answer reasonable?

   A Yes, he drove **about** 600 miles.

   B No, he drove **about** 550 miles.

   C No, he drove **about** 500 miles.

   D No, he drove **about** 650 miles.

Read each problem. Write your answers.

8   Sui Min wants to estimate the difference of 484 − 205.

   Part A

   What rounded numbers should she use?

   Answer: _____ and _____

   Part B

   Estimate the difference of 484 − 205.

   Answer: _____

9   Mrs. Wilson planted 52 daffodil bulbs, 25 tulip bulbs, and 34 iris bulbs in her garden. She figures she planted about 95 bulbs in all.

   Part A

   Is her estimate reasonable?

   Answer: _____

   Part B

   Use estimation to explain why or why not.

   _____

   _____

   _____

10 Midville Elementary School has 387 students.

   Part A

   What is that number rounded to the nearest ten?

   Answer: _____

   Part B

   The number of students at Princeton School rounds to the same number as Midville. What could be the number of students at Princeton School? Name all the numbers.

   Answer: _____

Read the problem. Write your answer for each part.

11   This chart shows how high some places in a park are.

SEVIEW PARK

Place	Height in Feet
Lakeside Cliff	483
Talon Hill	115
Hawk Mountain	436
Trail Park	207

Part A

What rounded numbers would you use to estimate the difference between the highest place and the lowest place?

Answer: _____ and _____

Part B

Anton estimated that the difference between the highest place and the lowest place is 300 feet. Is his answer reasonable?

Answer: _____

Part C

Explain why or why not.

_____

_____

_____

_____

Unit 5
Algebra, Patterns, and Functions

Algebra is a way to make general statements about relationships in math. You can use different symbols to show the relationships. You can also use patterns to show relationships. There are patterns all around you. The numbers on seats in a theater follow a pattern. The beads on a necklace might follow a pattern. This unit will help you use algebra and patterns.

Lesson 1 **Number Sentences** reviews how to use >, <, and = to write equations and inequalities.

Lesson 2 **Number Patterns** reviews how to read and understand a pattern that uses numbers. You will also find a missing number in a pattern.

Lesson 3 **Geometric Patterns** reviews how to understand a pattern that uses shapes. You will find a missing figure in a geometric pattern.

Number Sentences

Indicator 3.A.1 **CCSS** 3.NF.3.d

✔ An **equation** is a number sentence. It says two things are equal.

$$4 \times 5 = 20$$

This equation says, "4 times 5 equals 20."

✔ Sometimes a number in an equation is missing.

$$12 + \square = 20$$

This equation says, "12 plus some number equals 20."

To find the missing number, ask yourself what number added to 12 equals 20. Subtraction is the opposite of addition, so subtract to find the missing number: $20 - 12 = 8$.

The missing number is 8.

✔ An **inequality** is also a number sentence. It compares two things.

$$2 \times 3 > 5$$

This inequality says, "2 times 3 is greater than 5."

$$2 \times 3 < 12$$

This inequality says, "2 times 3 is less than 12."

✔ A number line can help you compare whole numbers and fractions.

Is $\frac{1}{4}$ greater than or less than $\frac{1}{2}$?

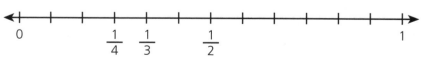

The fraction $\frac{1}{4}$ is to the left of $\frac{1}{2}$ on the number line. So $\frac{1}{4}$ is less than $\frac{1}{2}$: $\frac{1}{4} < \frac{1}{2}$.

Remember—

The two sides of an equation must **balance.** This means the sides are equal.

$$2 + 3 = 1 + 4$$

If the sides do not balance, the equation is not true.

$$5 + 1 \neq 2 + 3$$

This is *not* a true equation.

A box often stands for a missing number.

$$4 + \square = 10$$

Addition and subtraction are opposite operations. You can add to check subtraction.

$$17 - 8 = 9$$
because
$$9 + 8 = 17$$

The symbol $>$ means "is greater than."

$$2 + 3 > 4$$

The symbol $<$ means "is less than."

$$6 - 2 < 10$$

Read the labels on a number line carefully. They may be whole numbers or fractions.

Read each problem. Circle the letter of the best answer.

1 What number goes in the box to make this number sentence true?

$$10 + 6 < \square$$

A 14

B 15

C 16

D 17

> The correct answer is D. First add: $10 + 6 = 16$. The symbol $<$ means "is less than." So 16 is less than the number you must find. Look for a number that is greater than 16. Choices A, B, and C are all less than or equal to 16.

2 What fraction is less than point C on this number line?

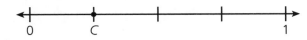

A $\frac{1}{5}$

B $\frac{1}{4}$

C $\frac{1}{3}$

D $\frac{1}{2}$

3 Which number goes in the box to make this number sentence true?

$$237 < 2\square8$$

A 0   **C** 2

B 1   **D** 3

4 Which number sentence is **not** true?

A $32 \div 4 > 3$

B $5 \times 7 < 20$

C $4 + 2 = 6$

D $30 - 20 < 16$

5 Which number sentence is true?

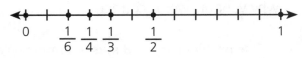

A $\frac{1}{3} < \frac{1}{2}$

B $\frac{1}{4} < \frac{1}{6}$

C $\frac{1}{4} > \frac{1}{2}$

D $\frac{1}{6} > \frac{1}{3}$

6 One parking lot holds 250 cars. A second parking lot holds 100 cars. These two parking lots together hold a greater number of cars than a third lot which holds 300 cars. Which number sentence shows the relationship among the parking lots?

A $250 + 100 < 300$

B $100 + 250 = 300$

C $250 + 100 > 300$

D $300 - 100 > 250$

Read each problem. Write your answers.

7 A number sentence says, "8 plus a number is greater than 21."

Part A

Write the number sentence. Use □ for the missing number.

Answer: _____ $8 + □ > 21$ _____

Part B

What number makes the number sentence from Part A true? Explain why your answer is correct.

> The problem says, "8 plus a number." You must add 8 to a number. So $8 + □$ is the first part of the number sentence. The second part says that it is greater than 21, so use the symbol $>$. You must find what number when added to 8 is greater than 21. The number 14 makes this number sentence true: $8 + 14 = 22$ and $22 > 21$. Any number greater than 14 also makes the number sentence true.

8 Look at this number line.

0   1

Part A

Draw point A on the number line above to show $\frac{1}{5}$.

Part B

Is $\frac{1}{2}$ greater than, less than, or equal to $\frac{1}{5}$? Explain how you know.

_____

_____

_____

Unit 5 Algebra, Patterns, and Functions

Read the problem. Write your answer for each part.

9 Mr. Hansen is baking cookies. He wants to set the oven to 375°F.

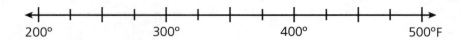

200°   300°   400°   500°F

Part A

Draw and label a point on the number line above to show 375°F.

Part B

Mr. Hansen set the temperature and waited for the oven to heat up. After 2 minutes, the oven was 315°F. Draw a point on the number line above to show 315°F.

Part C

Write an inequality to show the relationship of 375° and 315°.

Answer: _____

To find a **number pattern,** look at each number in order. Decide how the numbers change from one to the next.

What number comes next in this pattern?

2, 5, 8, 11, 14, ___?___

From 2 to 5 is 3. From 5 to 8 is 3. So the pattern shows counting by 3's, or adding 3 to each number. Add 3 to find the next number: 14 + 3 = 17.

The next number is 17.

What is the next number in this pattern?

5   10   15   20 ___?___

This pattern has a rule of "add 5." Add: 20 + 5 = 25.

The next number is 25.

Look at this pattern of numbers.

60, 50, 40, 30, ___?___, 10

To find the missing number in this pattern, ask yourself if the numbers get smaller or larger. In this list, the numbers get smaller. So you need to subtract to get the next number.

Start	Subtract 10	End
60	60 − 10 =	50
50	50 − 10 =	40
40	40 − 10 =	30
30	30 − 10 =	20
20	20 − 10 =	10

The missing number is 20.

> **Remember—**
>
> A **pattern** is a sequence that follows a set rule.
>
> If the numbers in a pattern get larger, use addition as the operation.
>
> 3, 7, 11, 15, …
> The rule is "add 4."
>
> 10, 20, 30, 40, …
> The rule is "add 10."
>
> If the numbers in a pattern get smaller, use subtraction as the operation.
>
> 85, 75, 65, 55, …
> The rule is "subtract 10."

Unit 5 Algebra, Patterns, and Functions

Read each problem. Circle the letter of the best answer.

1 Look at this number pattern.

2, 7, 12, 17, 22, ___?___

What number comes next?

A 24

B 25

C 26

D 27

> The correct answer is D. First find the pattern. Look for the difference between pairs of numbers: $7 - 2 = 5$, $12 - 7 = 5$, $17 - 12 = 5$. So the pattern is "add 5." To find the next number, add 5 to 22: $22 + 5 = 27$.

2 Look at the numbers on the beads.

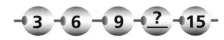

What number should be on the blank bead?

A 10

B 11

C 12

D 14

3 Look at this number pattern.

34, 29, 24, 19, 14, …

What number comes next?

A 13

B 10

C 9

D 3

4 Jenna is skip counting as shown below.

50, 41, 32, 23, 14

How is Jenna counting?

A backward by 9's

B forward by 4's

C backward by 4's

D forward by 9's

5 Which number pattern shows counting forward by 100's?

A 220, 270, 320, 370

B 220, 320, 420, 520

C 620, 570, 520, 470

D 620, 520, 420, 320

6 Look at the pattern of numbers on the parking spaces.

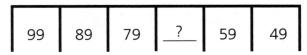

| 99 | 89 | 79 | ? | 59 | 49 |

What is the missing number?

A 75

B 70

C 69

D 65

Unit 5 Algebra, Patterns, and Functions

95

Read each problem. Write your answers.

7 A number pattern starts with 56. It follows the rule "subtract 6."

Part A

What is the fifth number of the pattern?

Answer: _____32_____

Part B

Explain how you found your answer.

> The pattern starts with 56 and goes down by 6 each time. So $56 - 6 = 50$, $50 - 6 = 44$, $44 - 6 = 38$, and $38 - 6 = 32$. The fifth number in the pattern is 32.

8 Tristan buys books for a price. He sells them for $4 more than he paid for them.

Part A

Tristan bought a book for $5. How much will he sell it for?

Answer: $_____

Part B

Explain how you found your answer.

_____

_____

_____

_____

Unit 5 Algebra, Patterns, and Functions

Read the problem. Write your answer for each part.

9 Look at this skip-counting pattern.

2, 6, 10, 14, 18, __?__, __?__, …

Part A

What are the next two numbers in the pattern?

Answer: _____ and _____

Ask Yourself
Does the pattern go up or down? By how many?

Part B

What rule describes the pattern?

Answer: _____

Part C

What would be the tenth number in the pattern?

Answer: _____

Geometric Patterns

Indicator 3.A.2

Patterns can be made with shapes or pictures. In some patterns, the shapes repeat. To find a **repeating pattern** in shapes, look at each shape in order. Find where the shape repeats.

What is the next shape in this pattern?

First there is a square, then two circles, then a triangle. Then the pattern repeats. The missing shape in the third set is after the two circles. So it must be a triangle.

In other patterns, the shapes grow in number. To find a **growing pattern** in shapes, look at each set of shapes in order. Decide how the number of shapes changes from one set to the next.

How many ☆ will be in the next set?

The first set has 2 stars. The second set has 4 stars. The third set has 6 stars. From 2 to 4 is 2. From 4 to 6 is 2. The pattern shows sets growing by 2's, or adding 2. The next set will have 8 stars (6 + 2 = 8).

☆ ☆ ☆ ☆
☆ ☆ ☆ ☆

Remember—

Sometimes a pattern uses a shape or picture that changes direction.

← ↑ → ↓ ← ↑ → ↓ ← ?

The arrows go left, up, right, down, and repeat. The last arrow points left, so the next one should point up, ↑.

A pattern can have two, three, or more elements before it repeats.

A B A B A B A B
A B B A B B
A B C A B C

A **shape pattern** can change by numbers, too.

○ ○○ ○○○ ○○○○

Unit 5 Algebra, Patterns, and Functions

Read each problem. Circle the letter of the best answer.

1 Look at the pattern on this piece of cloth.

What shape is missing?

A ★   C ●

B ▲   D ◆

> The correct answer is A. The pattern repeats after every four shapes (star, star, diamond, circle). The second star is missing in the pattern.

2 This picture shows the first four rows of a design.

Row 1 ♥
Row 2 ♥ ♥
Row 3 ♥ ♥ ♥
Row 4 ♥ ♥ ♥ ♥

Which picture shows Row 5?

A ♥ ♥

B ♥ ♥ ♥

C ♥ ♥ ♥ ♥

D ♥ ♥ ♥ ♥ ♥

3 Look at this pattern.

What comes next in this pattern?

A ☐   C ■

B ◨   D ⊡

4 The pattern shows two whole repeats.

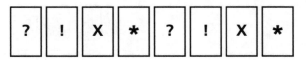

If the pattern continues, what will be the 13th symbol?

A `?`   C `X`

B `!`   D `*`

5 Look at this pattern.

What comes next in this pattern?

A   C

B   D

6 Look at this pattern of airplanes.

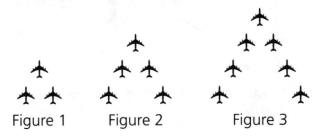

Figure 1   Figure 2   Figure 3

How many airplanes will there be in Figure 4?

A 8   C 10

B 9   D 11

Read each problem. Write your answers.

7 Tarrin arranged some cans in a display at a store.

Part A

If he makes the same pattern with six rows, how many cans will he need in all?

Answer: _____48_____ cans

Part B

Explain why your answer is correct.

> Each row has 2 more cans than the row before it. Rows 5 and 6 will have 11 and 13 cans. Add the number of cans in each row for the total: 3 + 5 + 7 + 9 + 11 + 13 = 48 cans.

8 Look at this pattern.

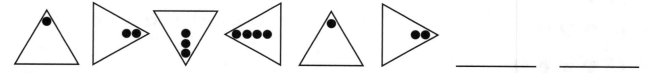

Part A

Draw the next two shapes in the spaces above to continue the pattern.

Part B

Explain how you found your answer.

_____

_____

_____

Unit 5 Algebra, Patterns, and Functions

Read the problem. Write your answer for each part.

9 Peter set up a display of boxes in a store window.

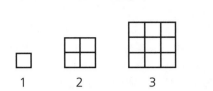

1   2   3   4   5

The fourth group of boxes was knocked down.

Part A

How many boxes were in the fourth group?

Answer: _____ boxes

Ask Yourself
How many boxes
are in groups 1, 2, 3,
and 5?

Part B

Explain how you found your answer.

_____

_____

_____

_____

Part C

Draw the sixth group of boxes below.

Read each problem. Circle the letter of the best answer.

1 The picture shows the first four rows of a pattern.

Row 1 ▢ ▢
Row 2 ▢ ▢ ▢
Row 3 ▢ ▢ ▢ ▢
Row 4 ▢ ▢ ▢ ▢ ▢

How many squares would be needed in all to make six rows of this pattern?

A 25   **C** 29

B 27   **D** 31

2 What number goes in the box to make this number sentence true?

$$20 + \square < 25$$

A 4

B 5

C 6

D 7

3 Look at this number pattern.

19, 17, 15, 13, ___?___

What number comes next?

A 12

B 11

C 10

D 9

4 Kelvin is skip counting.

9, 12, 15, 18, 21, 24, …

How is Kelvin counting?

A backward by 3's

B forward by 4's

C forward by 3's

D backward by 4's

5 Which number sentence is true?

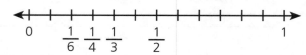

A $\frac{1}{2} < \frac{1}{3}$

B $\frac{1}{3} < \frac{1}{4}$

C $\frac{1}{4} > \frac{1}{6}$

D $\frac{1}{6} > \frac{1}{2}$

6 This pattern shows two whole repeats.

If the pattern continues, what will be the 15th letter?

A Ⓜ   **C** Ⓧ

B Ⓦ   **D** Ⓨ

Read each problem. Write your answers.

7 Look at this skip-counting pattern.

12, 23, 34, 45, 56, 67, __?__, __?__

Part A

What are the next two numbers in the pattern?

Answer: _____ and _____

Part B

What is the rule for the pattern?

Answer: _____

8 Langston scored 3 points higher than Penelope on a math test. Penelope scored 92.

Part A

Write an equation to find Langston's score. Use ☐ for Langston's score.

Answer: _____

Part B

Luke scored 97 on the test. Was Luke's score greater than or less than Langston's score? Write an inequality to show your answer.

Answer: _____

9 Look at this pattern.

 _____ _____

Part A

Draw the next two objects in the pattern above.

Part B

Explain how you know your answer is correct.

_____

_____

Unit 5 Algebra, Patterns, and Functions

103

Read the problem. Write your answer for each part.

10 Look at this pattern.

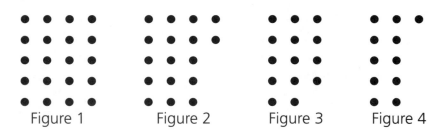

Figure 1   Figure 2   Figure 3   Figure 4

Part A

To make Figure 5, how many dots must be subtracted from Figure 4?

Answer: _____ dots

Part B

How many dots will Figure 5 have in all?

Answer: _____ dots

Part C

Describe how the pattern changes.

_____

_____

Unit 5 Algebra, Patterns, and Functions

Unit 6
Geometry

Look around you for a moment. You can probably find many examples of geometry. There are two-dimensional shapes. A poster on the wall might be a rectangle or a square. A paper plate is a circle. There are three-dimensional shapes. A shoebox is a rectangular prism. A can of soup is a cylinder. You can compare figures to decide if they are congruent or similar. Some figures have matching halves, which means they are symmetric. This unit will help you understand geometric figures.

Lesson 1 **Plane Figures** reviews two-dimensional figures like squares, triangles, hexagons, and circles.

Lesson 2 **Solid Figures** reviews three-dimensional figures like rectangular prisms, cones, and spheres.

Lesson 3 **Congruence and Similarity** reviews how to decide if figures are congruent or similar.

Lesson 4 **Symmetry** reviews how to decide if a figure is symmetric. You will also draw lines of symmetry on figures.

✓ **Polygons** are plane figures that have line segments for sides. Each kind of polygon has a certain number of sides and corners. The point where the sides meet is called the **vertex.**

A **triangle** has 3 sides and 3 vertices.

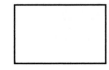

A **rectangle** has 4 sides and 4 vertices. The opposite sides are the same length and parallel.

A **square** is a rectangle with 4 equal sides.

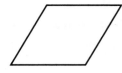

A **rhombus** has 4 sides that are the same length.

A **trapezoid** has 1 pair of opposite sides that are parallel. The sides can be different lengths.

A **hexagon** has 6 sides and 6 vertices.

Remember—

A **circle** is a plane figure but it is **not** a polygon. It does not have any straight sides.

The plural of vertex is **vertices.**

Parallel sides are always the same distance apart.

A square is a kind of rectangle with equal sides.

A **regular polygon** has sides that are the same length and angles that have the same measure.

An **irregular polygon** has sides that are different lengths. The angles are different measures.

Regular hexagon

Irregular hexagon

Read each problem. Circle the letter of the best answer.

1 Which of these shapes is *not* a triangle?

A

C

B

D

The correct answer is B. A triangle is a polygon with 3 sides and 3 corners. Triangles can look different, but they always have 3 sides. Choice B has 4 sides and 4 corners. It is not a triangle.

2 Levan drew this picture.

Which shape is *not* in the picture?

A square

B circle

C triangle

D rectangle

3 Which of these figures does *not* have 4 sides and 4 corners?

A trapezoid

B square

C rectangle

D hexagon

4 What is the name of this polygon?

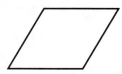

A triangle   C trapezoid

B rectangle   D rhombus

5 Which of these is a square?

A   C

B   D

6 What shape has 6 sides and 6 vertices?

A triangle   C trapezoid

B rectangle   D hexagon

7 Which of these shapes has sides of equal length and 4 angles of equal measure?

A rectangle   C hexagon

B square   D triangle

8 Which shape is a plane figure but *not* a polygon?

A   C

B   D

Read each problem. Write your answers.

9   Look at this drawing.

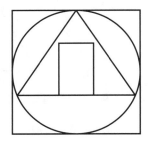

Part A

Name the plane figures in the drawing above.

Answer: _____square, circle, triangle, rectangle_____

Part B

Explain why your answer is correct.

A square (4 sides) is the outside shape. A circle has no straight sides. It is the first shape inside the square. It is followed by a triangle (3 sides) and a rectangle (4 sides).

10   Look at the shape below.

Part A

What is the name of the shape above?

Answer: _____

Part B

Explain how you know.

_____

_____

_____

Unit 6 Geometry

Read the problem. Write your answer for each part.

11 Cyrus drew these polygons.

1   2

Part A

Name each polygon.

Polygon 1: _____

Polygon 2: _____

Ask Yourself
How many sides does each figure have?

Part B

Explain how polygons 1 and 2 are alike and how they are different.

_____

_____

_____

_____

_____

Part C

Name one other polygon that has two pairs of opposite sides that are parallel.

Answer: _____

✓ **Solid figures** have special names.

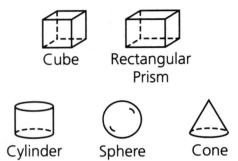

Cube   Rectangular Prism

Cylinder   Sphere   Cone

A **sphere** is a ball shape. A **cylinder** is a can shape.

✓ Some solid figures have flat faces that are plane figures.

A **prism** is a solid that has rectangles for the **sides** and two polygons for the **bases**.

This solid figure is a **rectangular prism**.

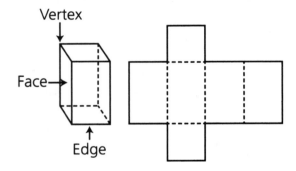

Vertex

Face→

Edge

Faces are the sides and bases of solids.

The **edges** are where the faces meet.

The **vertices** are the corners where the edges meet.

This solid figure is a **cube**. It is a kind of rectangular prism.

It has 6 faces, 12 edges, and 8 vertices. Four of its faces are rectangles. They are the sides. Two of its faces are squares. They are the bases.

This solid is a **triangular prism**. It has 5 faces, 9 edges, and 6 vertices.

Three of its faces are rectangles. They are the sides. Two of its faces are triangles. They are the bases.

6 Vertices

5 Faces→

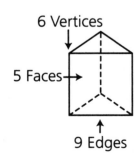

9 Edges

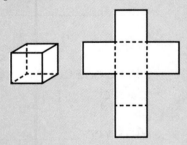

It has 6 faces, 12 edges, and 8 vertices.

A sphere has *no* faces. A cylinder has 2 faces that are circles. These faces are bases.

Read each problem. Circle the letter of the best answer.

1 What shape does a basketball have?

  A sphere

  B cone

  C cube

  D cylinder

The correct answer is A. A sphere is round and has a ball shape. A cylinder is shaped like a can, a cube is shaped like a box, and a cone has a flat bottom.

2 What shape are the faces on this solid?

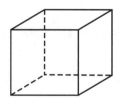

  A circle   **C** square

  B triangle   **D** rectangle

3 Which object has the shape of a cylinder?

  A TEA   **C**

  B   **D** BUTTER

4 Which solid figure has two flat circular bases and a curved surface?

  A cylinder

  B pyramid

  C sphere

  D prism

5 How many faces does this solid have?

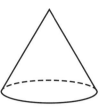

  A 0   **C** 2

  B 1   **D** 3

6 Which of these appears to be a prism?

  A   **C**

  B   **D**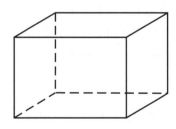

7 What are all the faces of this rectangular prism?

  A 4 rectangles

  B 2 squares

  C 4 rectangles and 2 squares

  D 3 squares and 1 rectangle

Read each problem. Write your answers.

8 Look at this solid figure.

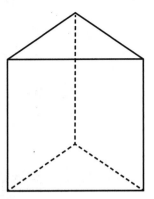

Name all the plane figures that make up its faces. Tell how many of each there are.

Answer: _____ 3 rectangles and 2 triangles _____

> This solid is a triangular prism. The faces on the top and bottom are triangles. The faces on the three sides are rectangles.

9 Look at these drawings.

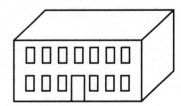 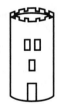 

Part A

Put an X on the building that has the shape of a cone.

Part B

Explain how you know your answer is correct.

_____

_____

Read the problem. Write your answer for each part.

10 Mrs. Chang bought these items at the grocery store.

   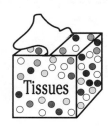      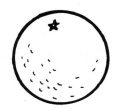

_____   _____   _____   _____

Part A

Label each item with the name of the solid it has the shape of.
Use these names:

cube   rectangular prism   cylinder   sphere

Ask Yourself
**What solid does
each item look like?**

Part B

On the lines below, explain why your answers are correct.

_____

_____

_____

_____

Part C

Name one other real-life object that is an example of each solid above.

_____

_____

_____

_____

Indicator 3.G.2

✔ **Congruent** figures have exactly the same size and shape.

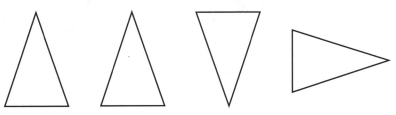

These triangles are all congruent.

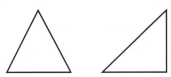

These triangles are **not** congruent.

✔ **Similar** figures have the same shape, but they may be different sizes.

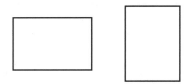

These rectangles are similar and congruent.

These rectangles are similar but **not** congruent.

These rectangles are **not** similar and **not** congruent.

Remember—

Two figures do **not** have to be in the same position to be congruent. You can turn or flip a figure and it will still be congruent.

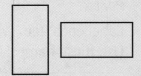

These rectangles are congruent.

114

Read each problem. Circle the letter of the best answer.

1 Look at this rectangle.

Which figure is congruent to it?

A    C

B    D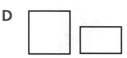

> The correct answer is C. That rectangle has exactly the same shape and size as the rectangle above. Choices A and B have different shapes. Choice D has the same shape but it is a different size.

2 Which of these is a pair of similar figures?

A   C

B   D

3 Which of the figures below are congruent?

1   2   3   4

A 3 and 4 only

B 1, 3, and 4 only

C 2 and 3 only

D 1 and 4 only

4 Look at this flower.

Which flower is similar to the flower above?

A   C

B   D

5 Kamila used a rubber stamp to make this design.

Which figure could Kamila have made with the same rubber stamp?

A   C

B   D

6 Arnold drew this shape.

Which figure is **not** congruent with Arnold's shape?

A   C

B   D

Read each problem. Write your answers.

7 Look at these trapezoids.

 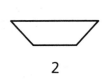
1   2   3   4

Part A

Which of the figures above are congruent?

Answer: _____ Figure 2 and Figure 3 _____

Part B

Which of the figures above are similar but ***not*** congruent?

Answer: _____ Figure 1 and Figure 4 _____

> Figures 2 and 3 are exactly the same shape and size. So they are congruent figures.
> Figures 1 and 4 are the same shape but different sizes. So they are similar figures.

8 Look at Figure 1 on the grid.

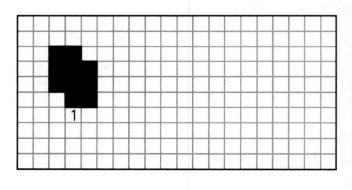

Part A

Draw a shape on the grid that is congruent to Figure 1. Label it 2.

Part B

Explain how you know your drawing is correct.

_____

_____

_____

_____

Read the problem. Write your answer for each part.

9 Katya cut out some cookies for her friends using cookie cutters. She wrote each person's name on a cookie with icing.

Part A

Whose cookies did Katya cut out using the same cookie cutter?

Answer: _____

> **Ask Yourself**
> What must be true about the shapes if Katya used a cookie cutter?

Part B

Explain how you found your answer.

_____

_____

_____

Part C

Are any of the cookies similar? Explain how you know.

_____

_____

_____

Symmetry

Indicator   3.G.5

✅ A figure has a **line of symmetry** if it can be folded so both parts match exactly.

 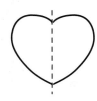

This figure has a line of symmetry.

✅ Some figures have **more** than one line of symmetry.

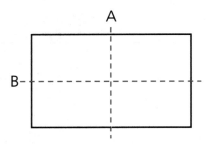

The rectangle can be folded on line A.

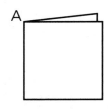

It can be folded along line B.

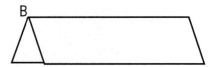

Some shapes have **no** line of symmetry.

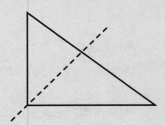

This is **not** a line of symmetry. If the triangle is folded on the line, the parts will **not** match.

Sometimes a line of symmetry is **vertical,** or up and down.

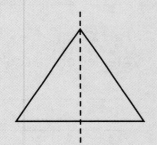

Sometimes it is **horizontal,** or across.

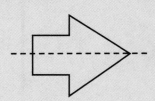

Read each problem. Circle the letter of the best answer.

1 Which figure has no line of symmetry?

A   C

B   D

> The correct answer is A. A line of symmetry divides a figure into exact halves. Choices B, C, and D will have matching halves when a vertical line is drawn through the center of each. Only the shell has no line of symmetry.

2 How many lines of symmetry does this figure have?

A   0

B   2

C   4

D   6

3 Which figure shows a line of symmetry?

A   C

B   D

4 Which of these letters has **more** than one line of symmetry?

A

B

C

D

5 Which of these shapes has the fewest lines of symmetry?

A

B

C

D

6 Which picture of the leaf shows a line of symmetry?

A   C

B    D

Read each problem. Write your answers.

7 Look at this figure.

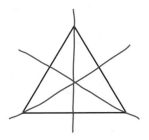

Part A

Draw the lines of symmetry on the figure. How many lines of symmetry does it have?

Answer: _____3_____

Part B

Explain how you found your answer.

> The triangle has 3 lines of symmetry, which cut the shape into matching halves. There is 1 line that runs from top to bottom in the center of the triangle. There are 2 lines that run diagonally across the triangle to cut it into matching halves.

8 Emmanuel drew this number.

Part A

Draw the lines of symmetry on the number above.

Part B

Explain why your answer is correct.

_____

_____

_____

Read the problem. Write your answer for each part.

9 This picture shows a canoe.

Part A

Draw all the lines of symmetry on the canoe above.

Part B

What will the figures on either side of the line of symmetry look like?

_____

_____

_____

Part C

Explain why your answer to Part B is correct.

_____

_____

_____

Read each problem. Circle the letter of the best answer.

1 Annette drew this picture.

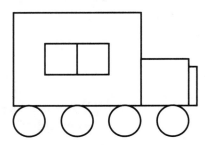

How many squares are in Annette's picture?

A   3   C   6

B   4   D   7

2 What is the name of this polygon?

A   triangle

B   hexagon

C   trapezoid

D   rhombus

3 Which shape has three sides and three vertices?

A   square

B   triangle

C   circle

D   hexagon

4 What shape are the faces of this solid?

A   rectangle   C   triangle

B   circle   D   square

5 Which object has the shape of a cube?

A

B

C

D

6 Which of these shapes has **more** than one line of symmetry?

A   C

B   D

Read each problem. Write your answers.

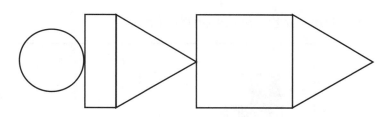

7 Look at the design at the right.

Part A

Name all the shapes in the design and tell how many of each there are.

Answer: _____

Part B

Explain why your answer is correct.

_____

_____

_____

8 Doug is playing a game. He tossed this game piece to see how many spaces he can move.

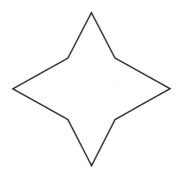

Part A

What is the name of this solid?

Answer: _____

Part B

What shape forms the faces of this solid?

Answer: _____

9 Look at the figure at the right.

Part A

Draw all the lines of symmetry on this figure.

Part B

Explain how you know your lines are correct.

_____

_____

Read the problem. Write your answer for each part.

10 Look at the figure on the grid.

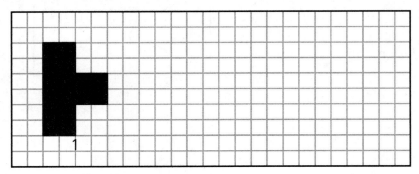

Part A

Draw a figure on the grid that is congruent to Figure 1. Label it 2.

Part B

Are Figures 1 and 2 similar?

Answer: _____

Part C

Explain how you know your answer to Part B is correct.

_____

_____

_____

_____

Unit 7
Measurement

Measurement is a math skill you use almost every day. When you go to the doctor's office, the nurse measures your height. This is like measuring length. Then the nurse measures your weight. If you have to take a liquid medicine, you must measure capacity. It is important to be able to measure things correctly. This unit will help you measure length, weight, and capacity. You will also estimate measurements.

Lesson 1 **Length** reviews how to use inches, feet, and yards to measure how long something is.

Lesson 2 **Weight** reviews how to use pounds and ounces to measure how heavy something is.

Lesson 3 **Capacity** reviews how to use cups, pints, quarts, and gallons to measure how much something holds.

Lesson 4 **Estimating Measures** reviews how to use personal references to estimate length, weight, and capacity.

Indicators 3.M.1, 2 **CCSS** 3.MD.4

✓ **Inches, feet,** and **yards** are customary units for measuring **length.**

| Use inches for short lengths. | Use feet for medium lengths. | Use yards for longer lengths. |

12 inches = 1 foot   3 feet = 1 yard

✓ To use a **ruler,** line up one end of the object with 0 or the beginning of the ruler. Find the whole numbers the other end falls between. Then decide what fraction of an inch it is closest to.

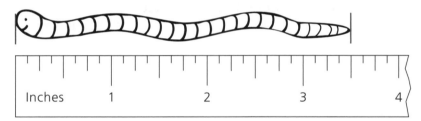

The worm is $3\frac{1}{2}$ inches long.

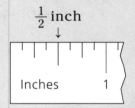

Remember—

Many times units of length are written with abbreviations.

in. = inch
ft = foot
yd = yard

Measure length using a ruler or yardstick.

The longest mark between numbers on an inch ruler stands for a half inch.

$\frac{1}{2}$ inch
↓

A **mile** is a customary unit of length. It is used to measure long distances.

Read each problem. Circle the letter of the best answer.

1  Use your inch ruler to help you solve this problem.

Which line is closest to $2\frac{1}{2}$ inches long?

A ▬▬▬▬▬▬▬▬▬

B ▬▬▬▬▬▬▬▬▬▬▬▬

C ▬▬▬▬▬

D ▬▬▬▬▬▬▬

The correct answer is B. To measure the lines, place your ruler so one end lines up with the beginning of the ruler. Then find the line that falls between 2 and 3. Choice A is $1\frac{1}{2}$ inches long, choice C is 1 inch long, and choice D is 2 inches long.

2 Which of these would you measure in inches?

A the width of a car

B the length of a paper clip

C the length of a soccer field

D the amount of soda in a can

3  Use your inch ruler to help you solve this problem.

How long is this chain?

A 1 inch

B $1\frac{1}{2}$ inches

C 2 inches

D $2\frac{1}{2}$ inches

4  Use your inch ruler to help you solve this problem.

How long is the pencil?

A 1 inch

B 2 inches

C 3 inches

D 4 inches

5 Which of these would you measure in feet?

A the length of a road

B the length of a trail

C the height of a sunflower

D the height of a doll

6 Which tool should Kehinde use to measure the length of his hand?

A a ruler

B a scale

C a thermometer

D a yardstick

7 Kevin wants to find how tall he is. Which unit should he use?

A inch

B foot

C yard

D mile

Unit 7 Measurement

127

Read each problem. Write your answers.

8  Use your inch ruler to help you solve this problem.

Look at this spoon.

Part A

How long is the spoon to the nearest $\frac{1}{2}$ inch?

Answer: _____ $4\frac{1}{2}$ _____ inches

Part B

Explain how you found your answer.

> Line up your inch ruler under the spoon. The end of the spoon measures between 4 and 5 inches. It is closest to $4\frac{1}{2}$ inches.

9 Trevon wants to measure the length of the school's football field.

Part A

Which unit would be **best** to use—inches, feet, or yards?

Answer: _____

Part B

Explain your answer.

_____

_____

_____

Read the problem. Write your answer for each part.

10 🔲 Use your inch ruler to help you solve this problem.

Luis is building a tree house. He has nails, like the one shown below.

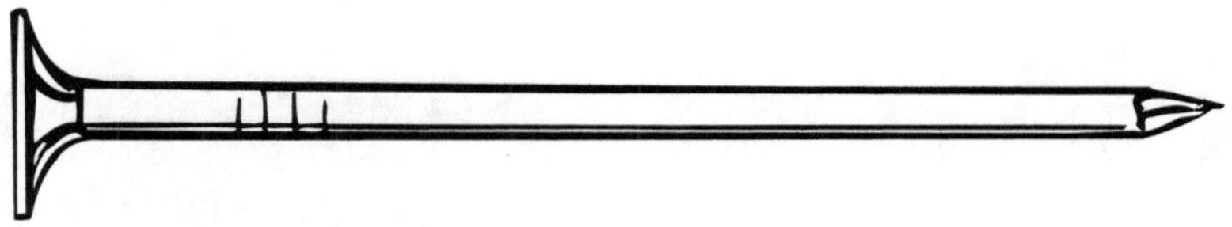

Part A

How long is this nail?

Answer: _____ inches

Part B

Luis has boards for the floor of the tree house. He has rope to use for the ladder. What unit should he use to measure the width of the boards—inches or feet? What unit should he use to measure the length of the rope—feet or yards?

Boards: _____

Rope: _____

Ask Yourself
What unit should I use for long lengths?
What unit should I use for short lengths?

Part C

Explain why your answer to Part B is correct.

_____

_____

_____

_____

Indicator   3.M.3

✓ **Ounces** and **pounds** are customary units for measuring **weight.**

A roll of candy mints weighs about 1 ounce.

A loaf of bread weighs about 1 pound.

16 ounces = 1 pound

✓ Weight is measured on a **scale.** To read a scale, first decide what the marks between the numbers stand for.

This scale is marked in pounds and ounces. The numbers stand for pounds. There are 16 spaces between numbers, so each mark stands for 1 ounce.

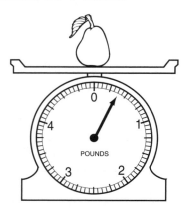

The pear weighs 6 ounces.

Read each problem. Circle the letter of the best answer.

1 How much does this sandal weigh, to the nearest ounce?

A   4 ounces   C   1 pound 4 ounces

B   14 ounces   D   4 pounds 1 ounce

> The correct answer is B. The pointer is between the 0 and 1, so the sandal does not weigh 1 pound. There are 16 spaces between numbers, so each mark stands for 1 ounce. The pointer is on the 14th mark, so the sandal weighs 14 ounces.

2 How much does the plant weigh, to the nearest ounce?

A   9 ounces   C   1 pound 9 ounces

B   29 ounces   D   2 pounds 9 ounces

3 How much do these tomatoes weigh, to the nearest ounce?

A   5 pounds

B   4 pounds 10 ounces

C   4 pounds 5 ounces

D   4 pounds

4 How much do the bananas weigh, to the nearest pound?

A   1 pound   C   12 pounds

B   2 pounds   D   22 pounds

Read each problem. Write your answers.

5 Aidan weighed this package at the post office.

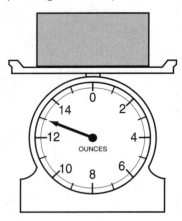

Part A

How much does the package weigh?

Answer: _____13_____ ounces

Part B

Explain how you found your answer.

> This scale measures ounces. Every other mark is labeled with an even number, so the marks without numbers stand for odd numbers. The pointer is halfway between 12 ounces and 14 ounces. So the package weighs 13 ounces.

6 Mr. Barzini is buying onions at the store.

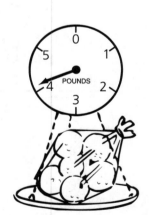

Part A

To the nearest pound, how much do these onions weigh?

Answer: _____ pounds

Part B

Explain why your answer is correct.

_____

_____

_____

Read the problem. Write your answer for each part.

7 Felix bought a piece of cheese for a family picnic. It weighed 3 pounds 4 ounces.

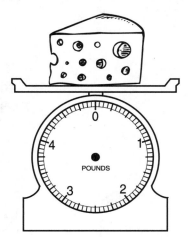

Part A

Draw the pointer on the scale to show the correct amount of cheese Felix bought.

Ask Yourself
Between which two numbers should the pointer fall?

Part B

Is this weight closer to 3 pounds or 4 pounds?

Answer: _____ pounds

Part C

Explain your answer to Part B.

_____

_____

_____

Capacity

Indicators 3.M.4, 5, 6

✓ Liquids and other things that flow are measured in units of **capacity.**

✓ **Cups, pints, quarts,** and **gallons** are customary units for measuring capacity.

Cup   Pint   Quart   Gallon

2 cups = 1 pint
2 pints = 1 quart
4 quarts = 1 gallon

✓ You can change a larger unit to a smaller one.

Joseph bought 2 gallons of milk. How many quarts is that?

1 gallon = 4 quarts
2 × 4 = 8 quarts

Joseph bought 8 quarts of milk.

✓ You can change smaller units to larger ones.

Kanye had 6 pints of orange juice. How many quarts is that?

2 pints = 1 quart
6 ÷ 2 = 3 quarts

Kanye had 3 quarts of orange juice.

Read each problem. Circle the letter of the best answer.

1 Hoshi wants to water some plants. Which container would she have to fill the fewest times?

    A a 1-cup can

    B a 1-pint carton

    C a 1-quart pitcher

    D a 1-gallon bucket

> The correct answer is D. A gallon is the largest unit of capacity, so it would hold the most water. Choices A, B, and C are incorrect because they are smaller units of capacity. Hoshi would have to make more trips to water her plants with those containers.

2 Which of the following is the greatest amount?

    A 5 cups   **C** 3 cups

    B 2 pints   **D** 3 pints

3 Which tool would be **best** for measuring the amount of water in a water bottle?

    A 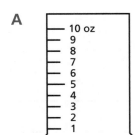   **C**

    B 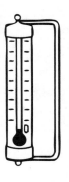   **D**

4 Mrs. Vandett is measuring the liquid shown below.

How much liquid is in the measuring cup?

    A 1 cup

    B 2 cups

    C 3 cups

    D 4 cups

5 Nick had 3 quarts of soda. How many **more** quarts of soda did he need to total 1 gallon?

    A 1

    B 2

    C 3

    D 4

6 Which amount would you measure using gallons?

    A cookies in a package

    B water in a bathtub

    C flour in a cake

    D bread in a loaf

Read each problem. Write your answers.

7 Gabriel bought 4 pints of apple juice. Trena bought 3 quarts of apple juice.

Part A

Who bought more juice?

Show your work.

$$2 \text{ pints} = 1 \text{ quart}$$
$$2 \times 3 = 6 \text{ pints}$$

Answer: _____Trena_____

Part B

Explain your answer.

There are 2 pints in a quart. Multiply the number of quarts, 3, by 2: $2 \times 3 = 6$. Trena bought 6 pints of juice. Gabriel only bought 4 pints of juice. So Trena bought more.

8 Ms. Syms needs to add milk to a pancake recipe.

Part A

Which unit would be better to use to measure the amount of milk she needs, cups or quarts?

Answer: _____

Part B

Explain how you knew which unit would be better.

_____

_____

_____

Read the problem. Write your answer for each part.

9 Each of these measuring cups holds 2 cups when full.

Part A

Clark is going to pour the liquid in all three measuring cups into the container shown below.

Ask Yourself
How much liquid is in each measuring cup?

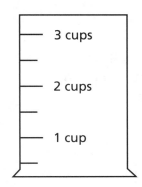

Draw a line on the container to show how full it will be after Clark pours in all the liquid.

Part B

How many pints is the liquid in the container from Part A?

Answer: _____ pints

Part C

Explain how you found your answer.

_____

_____

_____

Estimating Measures

Indicator   3.M.10

✓ Sometimes you do not need an exact measurement. Then you can use an **estimate.** An estimate is a number that is close, like a rounded number.

You can use **personal references** to estimate measurements.

What is a better estimate of the weight of an 8-year-old girl, 64 ounces or 64 pounds?

16 ounces = 1 pound

An ounce is a very small amount, about the weight of a large strawberry. An eight-year-old girl weighs more than 64 strawberries. So 64 pounds is the better answer.

✓ Here are some personal references you can use.

Units of Length	
Inch	diameter of a quarter
Foot	length of a man's foot
Yard	height from floor to a doorknob
Mile	length of 14 football fields

Units of Weight	
Ounce	weight of a key
Pound	weight of a loaf of bread

Units of Capacity	
Cup	a mug
Pint	a single-size serving soda bottle
Quart	a medium-size container of milk
Gallon	a small bucket

Remember—

Inches, feet, and yards are customary units of length.

12 inches = 1 foot
3 feet = 1 yard

Ounces and pounds are customary units of weight.

16 ounces = 1 pound

Cups, pints, quarts, and gallons are customary units of capacity.

2 cups = 1 pint
2 pints = 1 quart
4 quarts = 1 gallon

Inches and feet are **standard** units of measurement. They are always the same.

Objects like pens or coins that are used to measure are **nonstandard** units. They are *not* always the same.

Unit 7 Measurement

Read each problem. Circle the letter of the best answer.

1 **About** how much laundry liquid is used to wash one load of clothes?

   A 1 cup

   B 3 quarts

   C 8 cups

   D 10 gallons

> The correct answer is A. One cup of laundry liquid is a reasonable answer. Choices B, C, and D are amounts that are much too large for one load of laundry.

2 What is the **best** estimate of the length of a person's arm?

   A 1 inch

   B 2 inches

   C 1 foot

   D 2 feet

3 Kendall knows an inch is about the diameter of a quarter. If she uses a quarter to measure the length of this nail, what would be a reasonable estimate of the length of the nail?

   A 1 inch

   B 2 inches

   C 3 inches

   D 4 inches

4 What is the **best** estimate of the weight of a pony?

   A 10 ounces

   B 400 ounces

   C 10 pounds

   D 400 pounds

5 Which object could you use for a nonstandard unit closest to 12 inches?

   A the length of a sheet of paper

   B the length of a pen

   C the length of a paperback book

   D the length of a paper clip

6 What is the **best** estimate of the length of your shoe?

   A 1 inch

   B 7 inches

   C 15 inches

   D 3 feet

7 **About** how much milk does a milk carton hold?

   A 2 cups   **C** 1 quart

   B 1 pint   **D** 2 gallons

Unit 7 Measurement

Read each problem. Write your answers.

8 Look at this fork.

Part A

About how much would a metal fork weigh?

Answer: **about** ___1 ounce___

Part B

Explain why your answer is correct.

It would weigh about an ounce because ounces are used to weigh small objects. It is not heavy enough to be weighed in pounds.

9 Stacy said that 9 quarts of liquid is about 4 gallons.

Part A

Is Stacy's estimate reasonable?

Answer: _____

Part B

Explain your answer to Part A.

_____

_____

_____

_____

Read the problem. Write your answer for each part.

10 Stella estimated the width of her room as 4 feet. Stella's foot measures about 9 inches long. She took 10 steps.

Part A

Is Stella's estimate reasonable?

Show your work.

Answer: _____

Part B

Explain how you found your answer to Part A.

_____

_____

_____

Part C

What is a better estimate of the width of Stella's room in feet?

Answer: _____ feet

Read each problem. Circle the letter of the best answer.

1 Lyla has 5 quarts of grape juice to make punch for a party. How many **more** pints of grape juice does Lyla need if she wants to have 6 quarts of juice?

A 1   **C** 3

B 2   **D** 4

2 Which tool should Gracen use to measure the width of a car?

A a ruler   **C** a yardstick

B a scale   **D** a thermometer

3 What is the **best** estimate of the length of a car?

A about 1 inch

B about 15 inches

C about 1 foot

D about 15 feet

4  Use your inch ruler to help you solve this problem.

How long is this fish?

A $1\frac{1}{2}$ inches   **C** $2\frac{1}{2}$ inches

B 2 inches   **D** 3 inches

5 Which capacity is the smallest amount?

A 1 gallon

B 4 cups

C 3 pints

D 2 quarts

6 How much do the grapes weigh, to the nearest ounce?

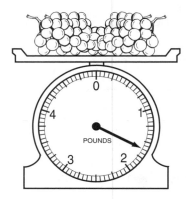

A 11 ounces

B 1 pound 10 ounces

C 2 pounds 1 ounce

D 10 pounds 1 ounce

7 Mr. Klein bought paint for his living room. What unit would be **best** to measure the amount of paint?

A feet

B yards

C pints

D gallons

Read each problem. Write your answers.

8 Use your inch ruler to help you solve this problem.

This picture shows a model of a riverboat.

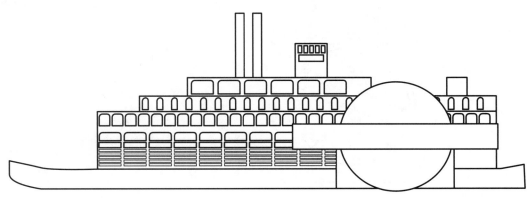

Part A

How long is the riverboat model, to the nearest $\frac{1}{2}$ inch?

Answer: _____ inches

Part B

Explain why your answer is correct.

_____

_____

_____

9 As part of his science experiment, Gary needs 4 cups of water.

Part A

How many times will Gary need to fill the measuring cup?

Answer: _____ times

Part B

Explain how you found your answer.

_____

_____

_____

Unit 7 Measurement

143

Read the problem. Write your answer for each part.

10 Rynell weighed this basket.

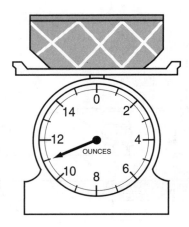

Part A

How much does the basket weight?

Answer: _____ ounces

Part B

Explain how you found your answer.

_____

_____

_____

Part C

Rynell placed 2 eggs in the basket. Each egg weighed 2 ounces. What is the total weight of the eggs and the basket?

Answer: _____ ounces

Unit 8
Time and Money

Look at the clock on the wall. You use a clock to tell time. Telling time is an important skill. It helps you know when to leave for school and when it is time for math class. It helps you know when your favorite TV show is on and when you have to go to bed. Everyone uses money. We use money to pay for things. We earn money for doing jobs. You must be able to recognize different types of money and count it. This unit will help you tell time and count money.

Lesson 1 **Money** reviews what bills and coins look like and how much they are worth. You will count a group of bills and coins to find how much money is there.

Lesson 2 **Time** reviews how to read different clocks to find the time. You will write time with words and numbers.

Money

✓ **Money** comes in **bills.** An amount of bills can be written in words or with symbols.

Twenty Dollars	Ten Dollars	Five Dollars	One Dollar
$20.00	$10.00	$5.00	$1.00

✓ **Money** comes in **coins.** An amount of coins can be written in words or with symbols.

Quarter	Dime	Nickel	Penny
$0.25 or 25¢	$0.10 or 10¢	$0.05 or 5¢	$0.01 or 1¢

✓ To find a certain amount of money, count the bills and coins.

What is the value of the money shown here?

There is one dollar bill ($1.00), one quarter ($0.25), one nickel ($0.05), and three pennies ($0.03). Add the total of each:

$1.00 + $0.25 + $0.05 + $0.03 = $1.33

The value of the money shown above is $1.33.

> *Remember—*
>
> The $ symbol is used before dollar amounts.
>
> $5.00 $8.27
>
> The ¢ symbol is used after cent amounts.
>
> 47¢   63¢
>
> There are two ways to show the amount of cents with symbols.
>
> thirty cents
> $0.30 = 30¢

146

Unit 8 Time and Money

Read each problem. Circle the letter of the best answer.

1 Tia counted the change in her pocket. She had 3 dimes, 2 nickels, and 8 pennies. How much money did she have?

A $0.42

B $0.45

C $0.48

D $0.51

> The correct answer is C. A dime is $0.10, so 3 dimes are worth $0.30. A nickel is $0.05, so 2 nickels are worth $0.10. A penny is $0.01, so 8 pennies are worth $0.08. Then add: $0.30 + $0.10 + $0.08 = $0.48.

2 Which of these is seven dollars and seventy-two cents?

A $7.0072

B $72.07

C $7.27

D $7.72

3 What is the value of the money shown below?

A $2.55

B $20.60

C $25.70

D $30.65

4 Which of these is equivalent to $1.00?

A 3 quarters, 2 dimes, and 1 nickel

B 2 quarters, 3 dimes, and 1 nickel

C 3 quarters, 1 dime, and 2 nickels

D 2 quarters, 3 dimes, and 3 nickels

5 Which of these is a way to write forty cents?

A $0.04

B $0.40

C $4.00

D $40.00

6 What is the value of the money shown below?

A $6.65

B $5.30

C $2.65

D $2.15

Read each problem. Write your answers.

7 The picture shows the money that Dante saved from his allowance.

Part A

How much money did Dante save?

Show your work.

$20.00 + $5.00 + $0.50 + $0.10 + $0.15 + $0.05 = $25.80

Answer: $____25.80____

Part B

Explain how you found your answer.

There is a 20-dollar and a 5-dollar bill. Each quarter is $0.25, so 2 quarters are worth $0.50. A dime is worth $0.10. A nickel is worth $0.05, so 3 nickels are $0.15. Each penny is equal to $0.01, so 5 pennies are worth $0.05. Added together, these sums total $25.80.

8 Briana bought a pack of gum for the amount shown here.

Part A

Write the amount of money in two different ways.

Answer 1: $_____

Answer 2: _____ ¢

Part B

Explain why your answer is correct.

_____

_____

_____

Unit 8 Time and Money

Read the problem. Write your answer for each part.

9 Xun got some money for his birthday.

Part A

How much did Xun get for his birthday?

Answer: $_____

Part B

Xun wants to buy some CDs with his money. They will cost thirty-nine dollars and fifty cents. Will Xun have enough money?

Answer: _____

Part C

Explain how you found your answer.

_____

_____

_____

Ask Yourself
What is the value of each coin and each bill?

Time

Indicators 3.M.8, 9 **CCSS** 3.MD.1

✅ A **clock** shows the time of day. The short hand points to the **hour.** The long hand points to the **minutes** after the hour.

This clock shows 4:15.

This clock shows 4:45.

✅ An hour can be broken into fractions of an hour. All the way around the clock face is 1 hour, or 1 whole.

Another way of saying 4:15 is "*quarter* after 4." That's because the minute hand has gone a quarter, or $\frac{1}{4}$, of the way around the clock face.

This clock shows 7:30. Another way of saying 7:30 is "*half* past 7." That is because the minute hand has gone half, or $\frac{1}{2}$, of the way around the clock face.

Remember—

A digital clock and an analog clock can show the same time.

Digital

Analog

1 hour = 60 minutes

30 minutes = $\frac{1}{2}$ hour

15 minutes = $\frac{1}{4}$ hour

Fifteen minutes before the next hour can be called "*quarter* to" or "*quarter* of" the hour.

10:45
quarter to 11

Unit 8 Time and Money

Read each problem. Circle the letter of the best answer.

1 Xavier walks his dog at half past five every evening. Which is half past five?

A  4:45

C 5:15

B 5:00

D 5:30

The correct answer is D. The word *half* is a clue. A full hour is 60 minutes, so half an hour is 30 minutes. Half past five is 5:30. Choice A is quarter to 5, choice B is 5 o'clock, and choice C is quarter after 5.

2 Gina leaves for school at this time every day.

What time does she leave?

A 3:25   C 6:45

B 2:35   D 7:13

3 What time does this clock show?

A 1:45   C 8:50

B 2:45   D 9:10

4 The deli stops taking orders at a quarter to ten. Which clock shows this time?

A    C

B    D

5 Which clock shows 12:38?

A    C

B    D

6 What time does this clock show?

A 4:15   C 3:22

B 4:02   D 3:15

151

Read each problem. Write your answers.

7 Brandon left for the store at 3:20.

Part A

Draw the hands on the clock face to show this time.

Part B

Explain why your answer is correct.

The short hand is after 3 but not yet at 4. The long hand, which shows minutes, is at the 4. That is 20 minutes after the hour. The clock shows 20 minutes after 3, or 3:20.

8 Look at this clock.

Part A

Write the time shown on the clock above.

Answer: _____

Part B

Explain how you found your answer.

_____

_____

_____

Read the problem. Write your answer for each part.

9 A flight from New York City to Buffalo is supposed to leave at quarter after ten.

Part A

Write this time on the digital clock face below.

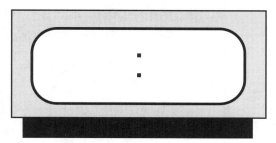

Ask Yourself
How many minutes past the hour is it?

Part B

Draw the hands on the clock face below to show the time.

Part C

Explain your answers to Part A and Part B.

_____

_____

_____

_____

Unit 8 Time and Money

153

Time and Money
Review

Read each problem. Circle the letter of the best answer.

1 What is the value of the money shown below?

A $15.41   C $14.15

B $11.31   D $20.26

2 Pablo left for his piano lesson at the time shown on the clock. What time was that?

A 8:21   C 5:45

B 4:42   D 7:18

3 Susan found 2 dimes, 4 nickels, a quarter, and 3 pennies in the bottom of her purse. How much money did she find?

A $0.59

B $0.66

C $0.68

D $0.71

4 The museum opens at half past nine every day. Which clock shows this time?

A    C

B    D

5 Which of these is equal to $1.00?

A 2 dollar bills

B 1 quarter and 4 dimes

C 4 quarters

D 1 dime and 7 nickels

6 Which is a way to write fifty cents?

A $0.05

B $0.50

C $5.00

D $50.00

Read each problem. Write your answers.

7 Jimmy went to sleep at 8:30.

Part A

Draw the hands on the clock face to show this time.

Part B

Explain why your answer is correct.

_____

_____

_____

8 The picture below shows the money Emma earned baby-sitting.

How much money did Emma earn?

Show your work.

Answer: $_____

9 Carlton bought a pack of crackers for the coins shown here.

Part A

Write the amount of money in two different ways.

Answer 1: $_____

Answer 2: _____¢

Part B

Explain why your answer is correct.

_____

_____

Unit 8 Time and Money

155

Read the problem. Write your answer for each part.

10 Runners began lining up for the race at a quarter of two.

Part A

Write the time on the digital clock face below.

Part B

Draw the hands on the clock face below to show the time.

Part C

The race began at the time shown below.

What time did the race start?

Answer: _____

Unit 9
Statistics

Number facts are data. You can find data in newspapers, magazines, and on the Internet. Graphs and tables help you organize data. This makes it easier for other people to read and to understand. There are different ways to show data. This unit will help you understand and make frequency tables, pictographs, and bar graphs.

Lesson 1 **Frequency Tables** reviews how to put data in a frequency table. You will also use tally marks to count data.

Lesson 2 **Pictographs** reviews how to use a graph with symbols to show data.

Lesson 3 **Bar Graphs** reviews how to make a bar graph. You will also use a bar graph to draw conclusions about things.

Indicator 3.S.3

✅ A **frequency table** shows how many or how often. It may use tally marks or numbers.

Tally marks are a way to record data as it happens.

How many times did Jerold win at tic-tac-toe?

TIC-TAC-TOE WINS

Player	Number of Wins
LaToya	⁄⁄⁄⁄ ⁄⁄
Jerold	⁄⁄⁄⁄ ⁄⁄⁄⁄ ⁄

Find the data for Jerold. Then count each group with a slash through it as 5. There are 2 groups of 5 and a single mark, for a total of 11. Jerold won 11 times.

This frequency table shows the same data as the table above. It uses numerals in place of tally marks.

TIC-TAC-TOE WINS

Player	Number of Wins
LaToya	7
Jerold	11

Remember—

Data is information in the form of numbers.

A tally mark stands for one thing or one time.

$$/ = 1$$

The fifth tally mark goes across the first 4 to make a group of 5 that is easy to count.

$$⁄⁄⁄⁄ = 5$$

Say:
⁄⁄⁄⁄ ⁄⁄⁄⁄ ⁄⁄⁄⁄ ⁄⁄
"5, 10, 15, plus 2 is 17"

Read each problem. Circle the letter of the best answer.

1 The table below shows the number of hamburgers sold in the cafeteria.

HAMBURGERS SOLD

Day	Number Sold
Monday	## ## ## ## ##
Tuesday	## ## ## ## ///
Wednesday	## ## ##
Thursday	## ## ## //

Which frequency table shows this data?

A
Monday	25
Tuesday	15
Wednesday	23
Thursday	17

C
Monday	25
Tuesday	23
Wednesday	15
Thursday	17

B
Monday	15
Tuesday	17
Wednesday	23
Thursday	25

D
Monday	23
Tuesday	25
Wednesday	15
Thursday	17

The correct answer is C. Count the tally marks by 5's. Monday shows 25, Tuesday shows 23, Wednesday shows 15, and Thursday shows 17.

2 Which table shows all the data from the frequency table below?

AFTER-SCHOOL PROGRAMS

Program	Students
Music	## ## ## ///
Art	## ## ## ## //
Sports	## ## ## ##

A
Music	20
Art	22
Sports	18

C
Music	18
Art	22
Sports	20

B
Music	18
Art	20
Sports	22

D
Music	22
Art	18
Sports	20

3 These sandwiches were in a machine.

Tuna	Ham	Cheese	Salami
Salami	Ham	Tuna	Cheese
Cheese	Ham	Tuna	Salami
Cheese	Salami	Ham	Ham
Ham	Cheese	Ham	Ham

Which frequency table shows this data?

A
Tuna	3
Ham	5
Cheese	4
Salami	8

C
Tuna	5
Ham	4
Cheese	8
Salami	3

B
Tuna	4
Ham	8
Cheese	5
Salami	3

D
Tuna	3
Ham	8
Cheese	5
Salami	4

4 Gunther has these marbles.

Which frequency table shows Gunther's marbles?

A
Color	Number
Red	4
White	2
Black	5

B
Color	Number
Red	4
White	5
Black	2

C
Color	Number
Red	5
White	4
Black	2

D
Color	Number
Red	2
White	4
Black	5

Read each problem. Write your answers.

5   Three students were running for class leader. Here are the votes each person got.

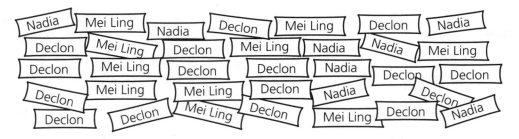

Make a frequency table to show the number of votes each person got.

CLASS LEADER

Name	Number of Votes
Nadia	8
Mei Ling	10
Declon	16

Count how many votes each person got: Nadia— 8, Mei Ling—10, Declon—16. Then place each person's name in the table and record the number of votes.

6   Hank planted flowers in his garden.

HANK'S GARDEN

Flower	Amount
Daisies	### ### ###
Zinnias	### ### //
Cosmos	### ### ### ///
Sunflowers	### ### ### //

Complete the table below to show the information in the frequency table above. In the shaded space, label each column correctly.

HANK'S GARDEN

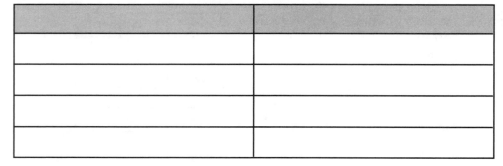

Read the problem. Write your answer for each part.

7 Classmates voted for their favorite baseball team. Here are the results.

Mets	Astros	Yankees	Mets	Yankees	Red Sox	Yankees
Red Sox	Mets	Yankees	Mets	Red Sox	Yankees	Mets
Mets	Red Sox	Mets	Yankees	Red Sox	Astros	Red Sox
Yankees	Astros	Mets	Red Sox	Mets	Astros	Yankees

Part A

How many votes did each team get? Make a tally using the data above.

Yankees: _____

Mets: _____

Red Sox: _____

Astros: _____

Ask Yourself
How can I keep track of each vote as I count it?

Part B

Change each tally into a numeral and complete the frequency table below.

FAVORITE BASEBALL TEAMS

Team	Number of Votes

Indicators 3.S.4, 5, 7, 8 **CCSS** 3.MD.3

✓ A **pictograph** uses **symbols,** or pictures, to show data.

To read a pictograph, look at the **key.** It tells how many each symbol stands for. Then multiply the number of symbols by the number in the key.

How many books did Vance read last year?

BOOKS READ LAST YEAR

Name	Number of Books
Chris	▢ ▢ ▢ ▢
Olivia	▢ ▢ ▢ ▢
Vance	▢ ▢ ▢ ▢ ▢

KEY: ▢ = 6 books

The key says that each symbol stands for 6 books.

Find the number of symbols for Vance: 5.

Multiply: 5 symbols × 6 = 30.

Vance read 30 books last year.

Remember—

You can also skip count symbols to find the total.

If 1 ★ stands for 2, count:

★   ★   ★   ★
"2,   4,   6,   8"

If 1 ■ stands for 3, count:

■   ■   ■   ■
"3,   6,   9,   12"

If 1 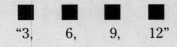 stands for 10, count:

"10,   20,   30,   40"

Sometimes a pictograph shows half of a symbol. Half of a symbol stands for half the number in the key.

Key: ★ = 2 stars
So ⟩ = 1 star.

Read each problem. Circle the letter of the best answer.

Use this pictograph to answer questions 1–4.

THIRD-GRADE STUDENTS

Class	Number of Students
Class 3-1	🧍🧍🧍🧍
Class 3-2	🧍🧍🧍🧍🧍
Class 3-3	🧍🧍🧍
Class 3-4	🧍🧍🧍🧍

KEY: 🧍 = 5 students

1 Which class has 25 students?

A 3-1   C 3-3

B 3-2   D 3-4

> The correct answer is B. The key says 1 🧍
> stands for 5 students. So think: What
> number times 5 is 25? 5 × 5 = 25. Look for
> the class with 5 symbols. It is 3-2.

2 How many students are in Class 3-4?

A 4   C 20

B 8   D 40

3 Which statement about the data in the pictograph is true?

A   More students are in Class 3-3 than in Class 3-1.

B   Fewer students are in Class 3-2 than in Class 3-4.

C   The same number of students are in Classes 3-1 and 3-4.

D   The same number of students are in Classes 3-2 and 3-3.

4 Suppose 10 new students enter Class 3-1. How many total symbols will be needed on the graph to show the number of students in the class?

A 7

B 6

C 5

D 4

Use this pictograph to answer questions 5 and 6.

BIRDS COUNTED

Week	Number of Birds
1	🐦🐦🐦🐦🐦🐦🐦
2	🐦🐦🐦🐦🐦🐦
3	🐦🐦🐦🐦🐦🐦🐦🐦
4	🐦🐦🐦🐦

KEY: 🐦 = 3 birds

5 What was the greatest number of birds counted in a week?

A 8   C 24

B 16   D 32

6 How many *more* birds were spotted in Week 2 than Week 4?

A 8   C 4

B 6   D 2

Read each problem. Write your answers.

7 Ajay collected 60 stamps. He wants to show this number with pictograph symbols.

Part A

If each symbol, 🖃, stands for 10, how many symbols should Ajay draw?

Show your work.

$$60 \div 10 = 6$$

Answer: _____6_____ symbols

Part B

Explain your answer.

> To find how many symbols are needed to show 60 stamps, divide the number of stamps by the value of the symbol, 10: 60 ÷ 10 = 6. Ajay needs to show 6 symbols.

8 Use the pictograph to answer this question.

ICE CREAM FLAVORS SOLD

Flavor	Number of Cones
Vanilla	🍦🍦🍦
Chocolate	🍦🍦🍦🍦🍦🍦
Strawberry	🍦🍦🍦🍦🍦🍦🍦🍦
Mint	🍦🍦🍦🍦🍦

KEY: 🍦 = 4 cones

Part A

What does the pictograph show?

Answer: _____

Part B

What does one symbol stand for?

Answer: _____

Read the problem. Write your answer for each part.

9 Ms. Madison kept track of the number of prizes her students won in an art competition. She made this tally table.

Pottery	*##\ /*	Painting	*##\ ///*
Drawing	*##\ ##*	Sculpture	*////*

Part A

Find the total number of prizes for each kind of art.

Pottery: _____ prizes

Drawing: _____ prizes

Painting: _____ prizes

Sculpture: _____ prizes

Ask Yourself
What does each tally mark stand for?

Part B

Complete the pictograph below to show the total number of prizes Ms. Madison's students won. Each X symbol should stand for 2 prizes.

ART COMPETITION PRIZES

Type of Art	Number of Prizes

KEY: =

Part C

On the lines below, explain how you knew how many symbols to draw for each kind of art.

_____

_____

_____

Bar Graphs

Indicators 3.S.4, 5, 6, 7, 8 **CCSS** 3.MD.3

✅ A **bar graph** uses bars to show data.

To read a bar graph, find the bar that stands for the data you want. Then look from the end of the bar to the number on the **scale.**

How many buses went to Buffalo?

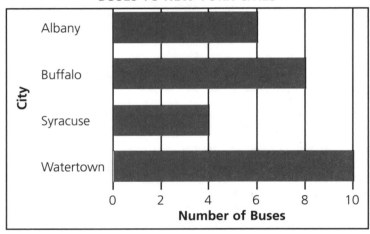

BUSES TO NEW YORK CITIES

Find the bar labeled "Buffalo." Then read down from the end of the bar to the number on the scale: 8. Eight buses went to Buffalo.

Remember—

The scale of a graph is the numbers on the side or on the bottom.

A bar that ends between numbers on the scale stands for a missing number.

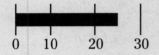

This bar ends halfway between 20 and 30. It stands for the number halfway between, 25.

The bars on a bar graph can be horizontal:

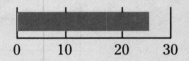

Or they can be vertical:

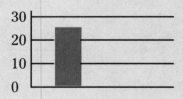

Unit 9 Statistics

Read each problem. Circle the letter of the best answer.

Use this bar graph to answer questions 1–3.

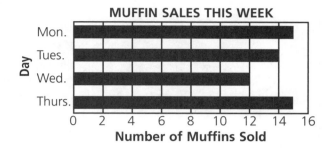

MUFFIN SALES THIS WEEK
Number of Muffins Sold

1 On which days were an equal number of muffins sold?

   A Monday and Thursday

   B Tuesday and Wednesday

   C Wednesday and Thursday

   D Monday and Wednesday

The correct answer is A. Find the end of each bar and read down to find its value. The bars on Monday and Thursday end at 15. So 15 muffins were sold on those two days.

2 Which statement is true?

   A More muffins were sold on Thursday than Monday.

   B There were fewer muffins sold on Tuesday than Wednesday.

   C The greatest number of muffins was sold on Tuesday.

   D The least number of muffins was sold on Wednesday.

3 A muffin sells for $1.00. How much money was made on Tuesday?

   A $12.00   **C** $15.00

   B $14.00   **D** $18.00

4 Some students were asked their favorite sneaker color. Here are the answers:

    black – 30   red – 20

    white – 10   blue – 25

Which graph shows the answers?

A

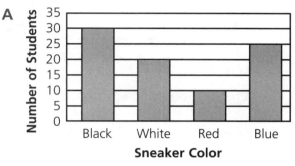

B

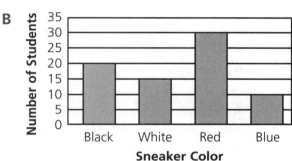

C

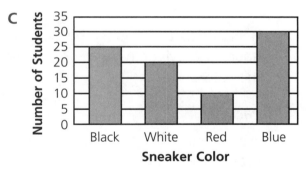

D

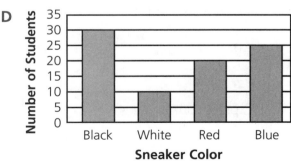

Read each problem. Write your answers.

5 Look at this bar graph.

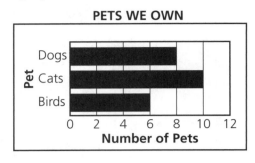

PETS WE OWN

Part A

What do the bars represent?

Answer: _____kind of pet_____

Part B

What do the numbers represent?

Answer: ___the number of each kind of pet___

> The graph shows the number of pets the students own. Each number stands for 2 pets. Each bar stands for the type of pet. The bars show that there are 8 dogs, 10 cats, and 6 birds.

6 Henry made this graph to show the number of hours of television he and some friends watched this week.

Part A

Henry concluded that most people watched **more** than 25 hours of television a week. Is this conclusion true?

Answer: _____

Part B

Explain your answer.

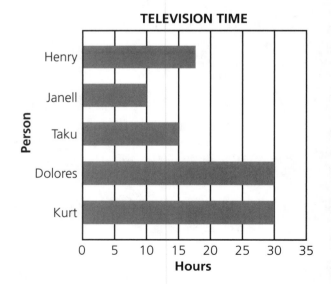

TELEVISION TIME

_____

_____

_____

Read the problem. Write your answer for each part.

7 Zara asked some friends where they like to go on vacation. Here are the results.

VACATION SPOTS

Mountains	
Beach	
City	

KEY: ☀ = 2 people

Part A

How can you change the data in the pictograph into bars for a bar graph?

_____

_____

_____

Ask Yourself
How many symbols represent the mountains? The beach? The city?

Part B

On the grid at the right, make a bar graph to show how many people like to go to each vacation spot.

Be sure to

- title the graph
- label the axes
- graph all the data
- provide the graph with a scale

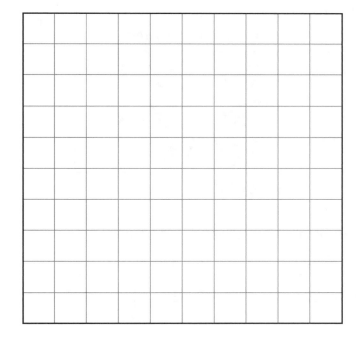

Statistics Review

Read each problem. Circle the letter of the best answer.

1 Students voted for their favorite lunch.

Pizza	⫫⫫⫫⫫⫫⫫⫫⫫ /
Tacos	⫫⫫ /
Burger	⫫⫫⫫⫫ //

Which table shows this data?

A

Pizza	6
Tacos	12
Burger	21

C

Pizza	21
Tacos	5
Burger	12

B

Pizza	21
Tacos	6
Burger	12

D

Pizza	20
Tacos	6
Burger	10

Use this pictograph to answer questions 2 and 3.

BUTTERFLIES AT THE PARK

KEY: = 10 butterflies

2 How many butterflies did Lee see?

A   25   C   15

B   20   D   3

3 Which statement is true?

A   Kendra, Lee, and Pedro saw the same number of butterflies.

B   Kendra and Lee saw the same number of butterflies.

C   Pedro saw the fewest butterflies.

D   Lee saw the most butterflies.

Use this bar graph to answer questions 4 and 5.

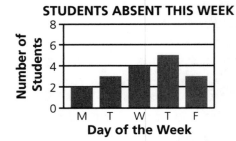

4 How many students were absent Thursday?

A   3   C   5

B   4   D   6

5 What is a conclusion that can be drawn?

A   There were at least 2 students absent every day.

B   The most students are always absent on Friday.

C   Some days there were no students absent.

D   Students don't like to be absent on Mondays.

Read each problem. Write your answers.

6 This pictograph shows the number of days four friends rode their bicycles in a month.

KEY: 🚲 = 4 days

Make a bar graph to show the data from the pictograph.

Be sure to
• title the graph
• label the axes
• graph all the data
• provide the graph with a scale

7 This graph shows how many glasses of water students drank on a hot afternoon.

Part A

Which two students drank the same number of glasses of water?

Answer: _____ and

_____

Part B

What was the total number of glasses of water the four students drank?

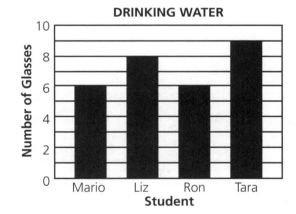

Answer: _____ glasses

Read the problem. Write your answer for each part.

8 A group of friends listed all the lakes they have visited in New York. Here are the results.

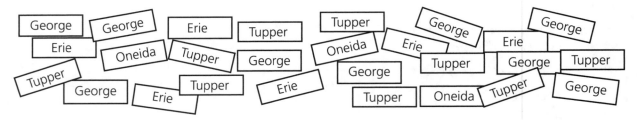

Part A

Make a frequency table to show the number of times each lake was visited. Show the tally for each lake. Change the tallies into numerals.

NEW YORK LAKES VISITED

Lake	Tally	Number of Votes

Part B

Use the information in the frequency table to make a pictograph of the same data. Draw check marks to show the number of votes.

NEW YORK LAKES VISITED

Lake	Number of Votes

KEY: ✓ = 3 votes

Unit 9 Statistics

Read each problem. Circle the letter of the best answer.

1 Oneida Lake is the largest lake in New York. It covers an area of about two hundred six square kilometers. Which number is two hundred six?

  A 206

  B 260

  C 2,006

  D 2,060

2 Which soccer jersey shows an odd number?

  A 24

  B 30

  C 36

  D 45

3 What shape is each face of a cube?

  A circle

  B triangle

  C square

  D trapezoid

4 Michelle flipped a coin 20 times. She wrote "H" for heads and "T" for tails.

T T H T H H H T H H
T T H T H T T T H T

Which table shows the number of heads and tails?

A

Result	Number
Heads	11
Tails	9

B

Result	Number
Heads	10
Tails	10

C

Result	Number
Heads	9
Tails	11

D

Result	Number
Heads	8
Tails	12

Read each problem. Circle the letter of the best answer.

5   The table shows the populations of three villages in Tioga County.

VILLAGE POPULATIONS

Village	Population
Spencer	731
Nichols	574
Candor	855

Which list shows the villages in order from greatest to least population?

A   Nichols, Candor, Spencer

B   Nichols, Spencer, Candor

C   Candor, Nichols, Spencer

D   Candor, Spencer, Nichols

6   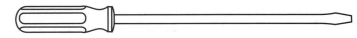 Use your inch ruler to help you solve this problem.

What is the length of this screwdriver?

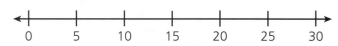

A   3 inches

B $3\frac{1}{2}$ inches

C   4 inches

D $4\frac{1}{2}$ inches

7   Look at this number line.

$$\xleftarrow{\quad}\overset{0\quad 5\quad 10\quad 15\quad 20\quad 25\quad 30}{|\ \ |\ \ |\ \ |\ \ |\ \ |\ \ |}\xrightarrow{\quad}$$

Which statement is true?

A $10 < 5$

B $20 < 10$

C $25 > 30$

D $30 > 20$

Practice Test

Read each problem. Circle the letter of the best answer.

8 Which number is the same as
500 + 40 + 7?

   A 547

   B 574

   C 745

   D 754

9 A cow weighs 425 pounds. A pig weighs 264 pounds. How much **more** does the cow weigh than the pig?

   A 161 pounds

   B 171 pounds

   C 251 pounds

   D 261 pounds

10 Mrs. Francis wrote this number sentence on the board.

$$8 \times \square = 0$$

What number goes in the box to make this number sentence true?

   A 0

   B 1

   C 4

   D 8

11 Which picture shows two similar shapes?

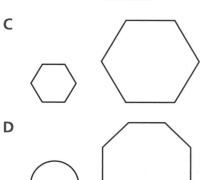

12 What fraction of this group of kittens is gray?

   A $\frac{1}{6}$

   B $\frac{1}{5}$

   C $\frac{1}{4}$

   D $\frac{1}{3}$

Read each problem. Circle the letter of the best answer.

13 There are 4 cups in 1 quart. Which measuring container has 3 cups of water?

A
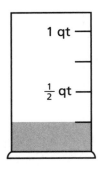

C
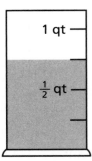

B
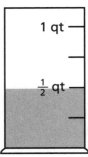

D
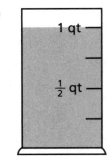

14 Use your counters to help you solve this problem.

Max wants to color one-half of these counters with a red crayon.

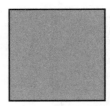

How many counters should Max color?

A   1

B   2

C   3

D   4

Practice Test

Read each problem. Circle the letter of the best answer.

15 Look at this pattern of squares.

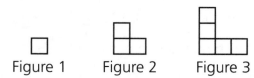

Figure 1   Figure 2   Figure 3

Which of these shows Figure 4 of this pattern?

A

B

C

D

16 A ranger counted 136 deer in the Catskill Mountains and 219 deer in the Adirondack Mountains. How many deer did the ranger count in all?

A 345

B 355

C 445

D 455

17 The picture shows a table at a restaurant.

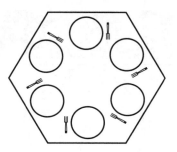

What is the shape of the table?

A square

B triangle

C hexagon

D trapezoid

18 Alicia pressed 52 leaves on Friday, 39 leaves on Saturday, and 31 leaves on Sunday. Which sum gives the **best** estimate of the total number of leaves Alicia pressed?

A 50 + 30 + 30

B 50 + 40 + 30

C 50 + 40 + 40

D 60 + 40 + 40

Practice Test

177

Read each problem. Circle the letter of the best answer.

19 How much does this dictionary weigh?

A 2 pounds 4 ounces

B 2 pounds 8 ounces

C 3 pounds 4 ounces

D 3 pounds 12 ounces

20 The pictograph shows the number of visitors to a circus each day.

CIRCUS VISITORS

Day	Number of Visitors
Monday	🧍 🧍 ⌐
Tuesday	🧍 🧍
Wednesday	🧍 🧍 🧍
Thursday	🧍 🧍 🧍 ⌐

KEY: 🧍 = 100 visitors

How many people visited the circus on Monday?

A 200

B 250

C 300

D 350

21 Karina is skip counting by 25's.

25, 50, 75, 100, 125, _____, …

Which number comes next?

A 126

B 135

C 150

D 175

22 There are 9 guitars in a music store. Each guitar has 6 strings. How many strings are there in all?

A 45

B 48

C 54

D 56

23 Which is the **best** estimate of the height of this pony?

A 5 inches

B 20 inches

C 5 feet

D 20 feet

Practice Test

Read each problem. Circle the letter of the best answer.

24 Which statement is true?

A $\frac{1}{2} = \frac{1}{3}$

B $\frac{1}{2} < \frac{1}{3}$

C $\frac{1}{4} = \frac{1}{5}$

D $\frac{1}{4} > \frac{1}{5}$

25 Which picture shows a cylinder?

A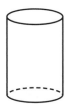

B

C

D

26 There are 28 students in Hannah's class. The teacher split the class into 4 equal teams. How many students were on each team?

A 6

B 7

C 8

D 9

27 The bar graph shows how many glasses of juice were ordered in a restaurant one hour.

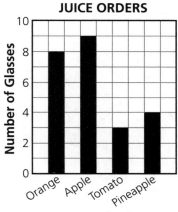

How many glasses of apple juice were ordered?

A 4

B 7

C 8

D 9

Read each problem. Circle the letter of the best answer.

28 Alejandro's piano lesson starts at 4:35. Which clock shows 4:35?

A

B

C

D

29 Jamar split his toy car collection into equal groups. Then he skip counted to find how many cars he has in all, as shown below.

5, 10, 15, 20, 25, 30

Which multiplication problem could Jamar do to find how many toy cars he has in all?

A 3 × 6

B 6 × 5

C 5 × 10

D 5 × 30

30 The table shows how many people climbed Mt. Marcy on five days.

MT. MARCY CLIMBERS

Date	Number of Climbers
June 1	20
June 2	24
June 3	28
June 4	32
June 5	36

If the pattern continues, how many people will climb Mt. Marcy on June 6th?

A 38

B 40

C 42

D 44

Read each problem. Circle the letter of the best answer.

31 A theater in Saratoga has 12 rows of seats. There are 12 seats in each row. How many seats are there altogether?

  A 104   **C** 144

  B 124   **D** 154

32 The picture shows the apples, bananas, and strawberries Mrs. Muldoon brought to a picnic.

Which table shows the number of each kind of fruit?

A

Apples	3
Bananas	4
Strawberries	5

B

Apples	3
Bananas	4
Strawberries	7

C

Apples	4
Bananas	3
Strawberries	5

D

Apples	4
Bananas	3
Strawberries	7

Read each problem. Circle the letter of the best answer.

33 What fraction of this circle is shaded?

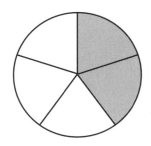

   A $\frac{1}{2}$

   B $\frac{2}{3}$

   C $\frac{2}{5}$

   D $\frac{5}{2}$

34 The driving distance from Buffalo to New York City is about 390 miles. What is 390 written in words?

   A   three thousand, nine

   B   three thousand, ninety

   C   three hundred nine

   D   three hundred ninety

35 Which picture shows two congruent shapes?

   A

   B

   C
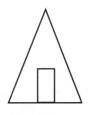
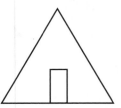

   D

36 Wayne cut a melon into 5 equal pieces and ate 1 piece. What fraction of the melon did Wayne eat?

   A $\frac{1}{6}$

   B $\frac{1}{5}$

   C $\frac{1}{2}$

   D $\frac{2}{1}$

Practice Test

Read each problem. Circle the letter of the best answer.

37 The picture shows the money George found in his drawer.

How much money did George find?

A $2.20

B $2.35

C $6.20

D $6.35

38 There are 128 cats in Mia's neighborhood. Of these, 81 of them stay indoors all the time. What is the **best** estimate of the number of cats that do **not** stay indoors all the time?

A 60

B 50

C 40

D 30

39 Which of these number sentences is true?

A 50 < 47

B 55 < 50

C 60 > 63

D 65 > 60

40 The bar graph shows the number of days it snowed in a certain town each year.

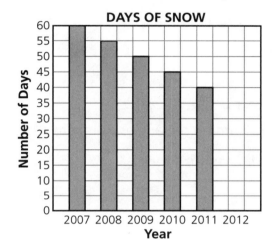

How many days will it probably snow in 2012?

A 45

B 40

C 35

D 30

Read each problem. Write your answers.

41 Look at this pattern of rectangles.

Figure 1   Figure 2   Figure 3   Figure 4

Part A

In the space below, draw Figure 5 in the pattern.

Part B

How many rectangles will there be in Figure 25?

Show your work.

Answer: _____ rectangles

42 Gabby had an odd number of flowers. Then she picked 9 more flowers.

Part A

Was the total number of flowers odd or even?

Answer: _____

Part B

On the lines below, explain how you found your answer.

_____

_____

Read each problem. Write your answers.

43 Arturo drew this shape on a piece of paper.

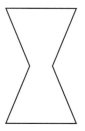

Part A

Draw two lines of symmetry on the shape above.

Part B

In the space below, draw another shape that has at least two lines of symmetry.

44 Look at this number sentence.

$$209 + 356 = 356 + \square$$

Part A

What number goes in the box to make the number sentence true?

Answer: _____

Part B

On the lines below, explain how you found your answer.

_____

_____

_____

_____

Read the problem. Write your answer for each part.

45 Juan drew this rectangle made of small squares.

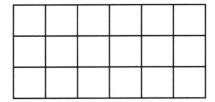

Part A

Use multiplication to find the total number of small squares in the rectangle.

Show your work.

Answer: _____ small squares

Part B

In the space below, draw a rectangle made of small squares to show the multiplication problem 4 × 5 = □.

Part C

On the lines below, explain another way to find the answer
to 4 × 5 = ☐.

_____

_____

_____

_____

_____

_____

Read the problem. Write your answer for each part.

46 The students in Mr. Conway's class kept track of the weather in February. The picture on each day shows the weather that day.

FEBRUARY

Su	M	Tu	W	Th	F	Sa
			1	2	3	4
5	6	7	8	9	10	11
12	13	14	15	16	17	18
19	20	21	22	23	24	25
26	27	28				

KEY: = Sun   = Clouds   = Rain   = Snow

Part A

Complete the table below to show how many days of sun, clouds, rain, and snow there were in February.

FEBRUARY WEATHER

Type of Weather	Number of Days

Part B

On the grid below, make a bar graph to show how many days of each type of weather the students recorded.

Be sure to
- title the graph
- label the axes
- graph all the data
- provide the graph with a scale

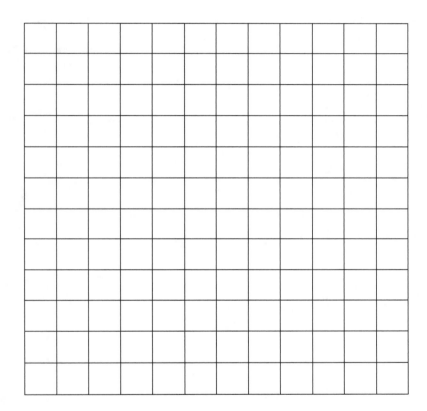

Glossary

A

add	operation used to combine numbers; uses the + sign
addends	numbers that are added in an addition problem to find a sum
array	a model using rows and columns of symbols or shapes
associative property	allows grouping of numbers with parentheses to be added: $a + (b + c) = (a + b) + c$

B

balance	to be the same on both sides
bar graph	a data display that uses bars to show data
bases	the faces of a prism or pyramid that can be any polygon
bills	paper money

C

capacity	the measure of how much liquid something holds
circle	a round plane figure with no straight sides
clock	a tool used to tell time
coin	a form of money: penny, nickel, dime, quarter
commutative property	allows numbers to be added or multiplied in any order: $a + b = b + a$ and $a \times b = b \times a$
compare	to decide which number is greater than or less than another number
compose	to put together
cone	a solid figure with one base that is a circle and a rounded side that meets in a point
congruent	figures that are the same size and shape

cube	a solid figure with six square sides
cup	a small unit of capacity in the customary system; about the amount of liquid in a mug
customary system	a system of measurement used in the United States. It measures length using inches, feet, yards, and miles.
cylinder	a solid figure with two bases that are circles. The bases are connected by a round side.

D

data	information in the form of numbers
decompose	to take apart
denominator	the number of parts in a whole or set; the number on the bottom of a fraction
difference	the answer in a subtraction problem
divide	operation used to split a group into smaller groups of equal size; uses the ÷ sign
dividend	the number being divided in a division problem
divisor	the number doing the dividing in a division problem

E

edge	where two faces meet on a solid figure
equation	a number sentence that says two expressions are equal
estimate	to make a good guess
even number	a number that ends in 0, 2, 4, 6, or 8; it can always be divided by 2
expanded form	a way to write a number that shows the place value of each digit

F

face — part of a solid figure that is shaped like a plane figure

factors — whole numbers that multiply to form a product

foot — a medium unit of length in the customary system. There are 12 inches in 1 foot.

fraction — a way of showing parts of a whole or of a set; shown as the number of parts being discussed over the total number of equal parts $\left(\frac{1}{2}, \frac{3}{4}\right)$

frequency table — a data display that uses numbers or tallies to show how many

G

gallon — a large unit of capacity in the customary system; the amount in a large jug of milk

growing pattern — a shape sequence in which the number of objects in each figure increases or decreases

H

halve — to divide in two equal pieces

hexagon — a plane figure with 6 sides and 6 corners

horizontal — goes across

hour — a unit of time. There are 24 hours in 1 day.

I

identity property — states that any number multiplied by 1 is always that number; any number divided by 1 is always that number

inch — a small unit of length in the customary system; about the length of a paper clip

inequality — a number sentence that compares two expressions; uses > or < symbols

inverse operations	operations that undo each other; opposite operations. Addition and subtraction are inverse operations. Multiplication and division are inverse operations.
irregular polygon	a polygon with sides that are different lengths

K

key	part of a pictograph that shows how many objects each symbol stands for

L

length	a measure of how long, wide, or tall something is
line of symmetry	a line that divides a shape into matching halves

M

mile	a customary unit of length used to measure distance
minute	a unit of time. There are 60 minutes in 1 hour.
money	bills and coins used to pay for things and services
multiply	operation used to combine groups of equal size; uses the $\times$ sign

N

nonstandard unit	a unit of measure that is not always the same
number line	a line that shows a set of ordered numbers, represented by tick marks
number pattern	a sequence in which numbers get larger or smaller according to a rule
numerator	the number of parts talked about; the number on the top of a fraction

O

odd number   a number that ends in 1, 3, 5, 7, or 9

operation   addition, subtraction, multiplication, or division

order   to arrange numbers from largest to smallest or from smallest to largest

ounce   a small unit of weight. There are 16 ounces in 1 pound.

P

parallel   always the same distance apart

parentheses   grouping symbols used to show order in a number sentence. Always do the operation inside parentheses first.

pattern   a sequence that follows a set rule

personal reference   an object that has about the same measure (length, weight, capacity) as a standard unit of measure; used to estimate a measurement

pictograph   a data display that uses pictures or symbols to show information

pint   a small unit of capacity. There are 2 cups in 1 pint.

place value   the value of each digit in a number

THOUSANDS	HUNDREDS	TENS	ONES
4	3	2	1

polygon   a two-dimensional figure with line segments for sides

pound   a medium unit of weight

prism   a solid figure with rectangles for sides and two polygons for bases

product   the answer in a multiplication problem

Q

quart   a medium unit of capacity. There are 4 quarts in 1 gallon.

quotient   the answer in a division problem

R

rectangle   a polygon with 4 sides and 4 angles. Opposite sides are parallel. The corners are square corners.

rectangular prism   a solid figure with 6 faces that are rectangles

regroup   to exchange 1 in one place for 10 in the place to its right, or 10 in one place for 1 in the place to its left; example: 2 tens can be regrouped as 1 ten and 10 ones

regular polygon   a polygon with sides that are all the same length

repeating pattern   a shape sequence in which a certain order of shapes repeats

rhombus   a polygon with 4 sides that are the same length

round   to replace a number with a close number that tells about how many or how much

ruler   a tool used to measure length

S

scale   a tool used to measure weight; the numbers on a bar graph

shape pattern   a sequence in which shapes or pictures change according to a certain rule

side   a line segment that forms part of a polygon

similar   figures that are the same shape, but not necessarily the same size

skip count   to count without saying every number; example: skip count by 2's: 2, 4, 6, 8, …

solid figure   a three-dimensional figure

sphere	a round solid figure, shaped like a ball
square	a rectangle with four equal sides
standard form	a number written as numerals
standard unit	unit of measure that is always the same
subtract	operation used to find a difference
sum	the answer in an addition problem
symbol	a picture that stands for something

T

tally marks	slashes used to record how many or how often
terms	the numerator and denominator in a fraction
trapezoid	a plane figure with 4 sides that has exactly 1 pair of parallel sides
triangle	a plane figure with 3 sides
triangular prism	a solid figure that has 2 bases shaped like triangles and 3 faces shaped like rectangles

U

unit fraction	a fraction with a numerator of 1

V

vertex	the place where two sides meet on a plane figure; plural: *vertices*
vertical	goes up and down

W

weight   a measure of how heavy something is

whole numbers   the counting numbers and 0: 0, 1, 2, 3, …

word form   a number written out as words

Y

yard   a unit of length in the customary system. There are 3 feet in 1 yard.

Z

zero property   states that any number multiplied by 0 is always 0

3 × 4 = 12
↑   ↑

3 × 4 = 12
↑

<

>

product	factors
greater than symbol	less than symbol
rectangle	triangle
rhombus	square

hexagon   trapezoid

cube   circle

cylinder   rectangular prism

cone   sphere

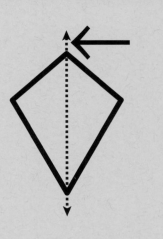

$\dfrac{1}{2}$ ←

$\dfrac{1}{2}$ ←

$3 \times 5 = 5 \times 3$

$2 + (3 + 5) = (2 + 3) + 5$

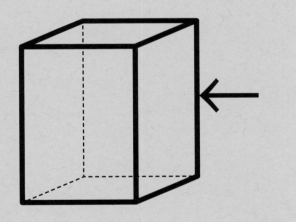

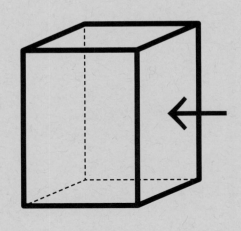

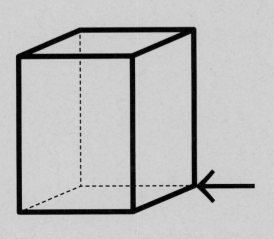

numerator

line of
symmetry

commutative
property of
multiplication

denominator

edge

associative
property of
addition

vertex

face